A TRAIN TO CATCH

A TRAIN TO CATCH

A RETURN TICKET TO THE GOLDEN AGE OF FISHING

JON BERRY

ELLESMERE

THE MEDLAR PRESS

2011

Published by The Medlar Press Limited,
The Grange, Ellesmere, Shropshire.
www.medlarpress.com

ISBN 978-1-907110-31-3

Text © Jon Berry 2011
Design © The Medlar Press 2011
Cover Photograph © Andrew Herd
Other photographs by Jon Berry, Andrew Herd and Jon Ward-Allen

Jon Berry has asserted his rights
under the Copyright, Design and Patents Act, 1988,
to be identified as Author of this work.

*Considerable thanks are due to the individuals mentioned in this book.
Each of them helped turn a journey into a story, and this book could not have
been written without them. Less gratitude is extended to the modern railway
companies who (with the admirable exception of East Anglian) showed far less
interest in travelling anglers than their Victorian and Edwardian predecessors.
I will, however, apologise to each of them for using their carriages, and
hope that any lingering aroma of trout pellets or wet nets
reminds them of the glory days.*

Produced in England by The Medlar Press Limited, Ellesmere.
Designed and typeset in 12 on 15pt Bembo Roman.

Contents

Introduction

Before the railways arrived in the first half of the nineteenth-century, the travelling angler was limited to waters to which he could walk, sail or ride. Fishing was, for the majority, a local pastime done with either food or sport in mind. All this changed through a succession of human triumphs - James Watt's steam engine, the early locomotives of Trevithick and Stephenson, the vision of men like William James for a new kind of industry; each of these altered the landscape, physically and socially. By the middle years of Victoria's century, a new railway network had stretched to all corners of Great Britain.

The large rail companies were smart in recognising the demand for tickets among the nation's fishermen. City dwelling anglers were keen to escape the belching fug of the industrial age and find peace by water, and the railway companies were happy to take them there. Privilege tickets were negotiated with the great angling clubs and stations soon appeared at prime fishing spots. The age of the railway angler had arrived.

But why follow them now, more than a century later? The cuts of Richard Beeching in the 1960s anticipated the growth of the motor car, and many -

A BLANK DAY

Old Gent (greeting friend). " Hullo, Jorkins ! 'Been
fishing ? What did you catch ? "
Jorkins (gloomily). " Ha'-past six train home ! "

perhaps most - of those little riverside stations have
gone. Saturday mornings at Liverpool Street and
Paddington no longer bring crowds of men, creels and
rods by their sides, waiting for the early train to a
greener, pleasanter land. The salmon-chasing gentry
no longer instruct their man to stack the Pall Mall rod

boxes to the rear of their private carriage and fix them a gin while they're at it. Fishing has, in a curious way, been democratised by the decline in rail travel. Now every one of us - working man and playboy, carp addict and dry-fly purist - jumps into a car and ploughs the common furrow of the motorway.

And that, perhaps, is the point. Fishing itself has not lost its charm; the everyday miracles of rising trout or disappearing floats are as potent as ever. But the way in which we go about it, and the landscape in which we do it, have changed beyond all recognition in the century-and-a-half since we abandoned our farms for factories. The journey to the water is now one of efficiency and solitude and, for me, has lost something in the process. The chattering pixels of the Sat Nav have replaced the view from the carriage window. More fool us.

These journeys took place over three years. Both the publisher and I would have liked this to have been one long, circuitous tour, but the demands of my 'real' work - teaching in a Swindon secondary school - and the financial constraints upon publishers, not to mention teachers, made that impossible. And so I took these journeys just as the Victorians and Edwardians would have done, as a sequence of holidays. We planned a variety of excursions which would cover much of the British mainland, from the south-west to the Highlands, Wales to East Anglia, and we very nearly stuck to it. There were adventures which were planned but that never happened - with the barbel of

the Trent, the tench of Blenheim Palace, the wonderful trout of Blagdon - but those that did were all to popular destinations in the golden era of the railways. There were times when those routes came to an undignified end, days on which I cursed Beeching and had to find another way to the water, but that was the point too - to see if it could still be done. The occasions when I borrowed a car, or hailed a taxi, were borne of necessity rather than convenience. I promise.

When the first journey took place, I owned two of the old fishing guides which the railway companies issued to attract customers. They were called *Haunts and Hints for Anglers* and were published by the GWR (Great Western Railways) in the 1920s. In the months that followed, I came across many more of these guides, and some of their words and pictures are included here, to give a flavour of the new, expansive world in which our predecessors found themselves. For me, they show an innocence and generosity of spirit that is all but gone - but that is worth remembering. I hope you like them.

When the publisher first suggested that I write this book, the idea appealed to me on a very personal level. My earliest forays with a rod came during holidays to Scotland, at the end of long journeys on the night-sleeper from London with my mother and brother. Because of those summer holiday jaunts to the Highlands, my fishing has always been about going somewhere else - geographically or otherwise. And from the age of five until now, the smell of oiled engines and the blow of a station-master's whistle remind me of small brown trout. I know it is a bit odd, but there we are; a century earlier, such associations would have been quite usual.

Many people helped me to make these journeys and to catch some fish along the way. With several thousand miles of tracks behind me, and a few decent catches too, the task of thanking them all here is an onerous one – and one which I shall therefore dodge. They are all mentioned within these pages and they know who they are. To all of you, I am sincerely grateful.

Negley Farson, in his indecently good *Going Fishing*, said that the fisherman's reward was the spots his sport took him to. Farson was right, of course. I would add only one minor caveat to this; there is reward too in how we get there and what we see along the way. I hope you enjoy these journeys.

Jon Berry, October 2011

Chapter I

The Peacock

Grand tours have to start somewhere. That said, few people would choose to start theirs on a rain-soaked platform in Swindon - the town that gave us Billie Piper, Diana Dors and the Great Western Railway. Even its staunchest advocates would accept that Swindon is not the most salubrious of places, and it might never have existed but for the actions of two men. In the 1860s Isambard Kingdom Brunel and Daniel Gooch chose the flat land below the pig farms of Old Swinedown as the site for GWR's workshop and station, and a new settlement was born. It grew rapidly, as men moved from Wales and the North to find work building engines and carriages. Railway workers' cottages line the tracks to this day, and some of the GWR buildings remain, but the excesses of the twenty-first century have now claimed this part of town; the golden age of steam - days when anglers boarded trains clutching second or third class tickets and wicker creels - cannot easily be imagined among the syringes and working girls of Manchester

Road or the high rise offices of the business district to the south. Nevertheless, when my railway odyssey began Swindon was home, and I had to begin somewhere.

The premise behind my journey was a simple one. Between the 1860s and the 1930s, railway companies across Britain recognised the popularity of angling and provided trains to take its followers to river, lake and sea. Cut-price tickets were offered to members of the great angling clubs, and the railway companies even published guidebooks to the best fishing spots around the country. Sunday mornings would see thousands of 'soldiers of the taper lance', to use J. P. Wheeldon's evocative phrase, gathering on platforms from London to Inverness in search of a day's sport. For the better-off fisher, luxurious carriages were available to escort them out of the capital and northwards to the salmon of Scotland. Anglers' Trains reached every corner of mainland Britain, and it was only the advent of the motor car - and later the ruthless rationalising of the rail network by Richard Beeching - which killed off this sublime tradition. I wanted to follow some of their journeys, catch a few fish, and see if their world could be glimpsed in ours.

By lunchtime I was expected by an angling pal in one of Derbyshire's oldest fishing inns, the Peacock Hotel at Rowsley. A well-organised Victorian would no doubt have journeyed the night before, perhaps staying in one of the station hotels, but the hotels have gone and it was cheaper to take the early morning train - waving one's fishing club card around doesn't merit a discount any more.

The first train took me to Cheltenham Spa and its delightful 1840s station, where there was a forty-minute

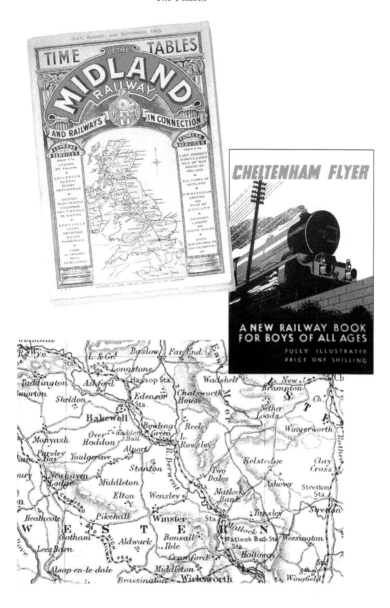

wait. Sadly, I didn't have a copy of *Cheltenham Flyer* with me to while away the time (published by GWR in 1932 to encourage 'boys of all ages to take an interest in railways'), so I decided to absorb a little local culture instead. I followed the signs outside the station to Rick's Café, on an industrial estate behind the old Midland Hotel - once a well-appointed stopping point for weary rail travellers, but now a pub boasting Live TV Football and a Games Room.

The eponymous café owner was in a talkative mood, and deduced from my rod and net that I was going fishing. I explained that I was doing a little more than that, and that this was my first stop on a grand tour by rail that might eventually appear in print. "By train? You're a bloody idiot, mate. It'll cost a fortune," he said. I agreed, and paid for breakfast, knowing that he had already (incorrectly) sized me up as having more money than sense.

By midday I'd crossed rivers as diverse as the Bristol Avon, the Warwickshire Avon, the Dove and the Trent. I'd fished all of them in the past, usually for barbel and pike, and always with the comfort of a car to take me there. The perspective from a train's carriage felt somehow different, though at this point in the adventure it was too early to articulate what that difference was. There was no urgency; I had two years and ten thousand miles to figure it out.

It did occur to me - with far greater clarity - that it was still raining. I bought a rejuvenating coffee from a machine on the platform at Derby, but it tasted like floodwater. No matter - there were clearer skies in the north-west, and the prospect of wild trout became very real.

A third, brief journey took me as far as Matlock. Like so many stations I would visit in the course of these journeys, it suffered at the hands of Richard Beeching, and was reduced to a single track in 1968. It was here that my carefully-planned first day began to unravel. I had intended to dash over the road to a private steam railway running alongside the Derwent, and make my dramatic entrance to Rowsley on Peak Rails' WD150 Royal Pioneer - a proper, puffing behemoth boasting an Austerity 0-6-0 wheelbase and saddle tank design, according to the guidebooks. Yorkie would be there with his camera to capture my emergence from the steam, and the finest digital software would conjure a silhouette of man, rod and creel against the backdrop of an old steam train. Before a line had been cast or a word written, the front cover would be in the can. All I had to do was be on the train . . . but I missed it.

This was not entirely my fault. There appears to be something of a schism between BR at Matlock station and the enthusiasts trying to revive the old Derwent Line - nothing serious, not a families ripped asunder civil war sort of split, more a Women's Institute tiff over tea money, but a schism nonetheless. The former denied any association with the latter and were less than helpful in offering directions, and I missed the Royal Pioneer by a matter of minutes. My eventual arrival in Rowsley - sat in the 'pushchairs only' section of a Transpeak bus, next to a hyperventilating old boy who wanted to discuss 'them babelfish below that bridge at Matlock' - was less than momentous. Certainly not the stuff of front covers.

It was, of course, still raining when I walked in to the Peacock Hotel and met Yorkie and his friend Richard.

THE PEACOCK HOTEL. This is a picturesque hostelry, in the pretty village of Rowsley, near Matlock, Derbyshire, and well known throughout the country as a favourite resort of the angler, and as a very comfortable home for the tourist, in those picturesque localities.

I've known the former for many years. His nom de plume hints at his county of birth rather than any similarity to a chocolate bar, and makes his allegiance to Manchester United even less justifiable, but he's a good fisherman and even better company and I was pleased to see him. Richard was our host and we'd not met before. Both had steaming mugs of coffee in front of them, and were busily playing with cameras and looking at photographs they'd just taken of the Royal Pioneer - the photographs I was supposed to be in, but wasn't. I wanted lunch, and perhaps a beer. Neither was possible - we were going fishing.

The Peacock Hotel water on the Derbyshire Wye has been a historic trout fishery since the early 1800s. The river itself, which encompasses 7½ miles of the Wye and shorter stretches of its two tributaries, the Lathkill and

Bradford, has been part of the Haddon Estate for some eight hundred years. Day tickets have been available from the Peacock Hotel or directly from the estate since 1820, and the fishery has been dry-fly only since 1865. The current Head River Keeper, Warren Slaney, practises a policy of wild fish only; no trout or eggs have been introduced to the river since 2003, and my hosts assured me that the browns were of outstanding quality. The Wye is also the only English river where rainbow trout thrive naturally. The Victorians introduced them, but this stocking ceased years ago and since then they have bred successfully, and now live alongside the browns and grayling. If I caught one, Richard told me, it would be unlike any triploid stockie I'd ever encountered.

Among trout fishers in-the-know the Wye at Rowsley is famous water, and has been for two centuries. The Peacock Hotel's water featured regularly in nineteenth and early-twentieth century angling literature. W. Adams wrote of it in his *Derbyshire Dales and Fishing Streams* (1861), as did Raymond Hill in *Wings and Hackles* and A. Nelson Bromley in *A Fly-Fisher's Reflections* (1930). More recently, whenever the monthly magazines publish their 'fifty places you must catch a trout if you want to be regarded as a proper fly fisherman and not a bungling amateur'-type articles, the Wye is there. I'm anything but 'in-the-know', but even I knew about it.

There are more famous trout streams, of course, especially further south in the waters of Halford and Skues, but part of the Wye's reputation can be explained by its accessibility. Anyone can fish it, and day-ticket prices are far below those on top beats of the Test or Itchen. Consequently, the Wye at Rowsley attracts visitors from all over the country. It has long been so, and in the later years of Victoria's reign the weekly angling journals often featured correspondence between prospective visitors to the Wye and local anglers.

I read some of these letters during an afternoon at the National Newspaper Library in Colindale – which, incidentally, is one of the finest institutions in the known universe, and conclusive proof that not everything in the capital had gone to the dogs. The following is typical:

Sir – replying to C.H.O.'s letter in your last issue, the best months for fishing the Wye are April, May and September for trout, and during the summer months the evening fishing is A1. Average baskets from four to six brace. I have always found small flies fished upstream to kill best. The flies I obtain from W. Chalmers, 15, Marcus Street, Hulme, Manchester, from whom all practical information can be obtained. – Black Spider (Fishing, 6th March, 1886)

The river was popular with local anglers, but many came by train from Manchester to catch its trout and grayling. The Manchester Anglers' Association published two books entitled *Anglers' Evenings* consisting of essays by its members, in 1880 and 1882. Both editions included chapters about the Wye's trout and grayling, and I had taken my copies along to show Richard. David Reid's opening paragraphs from the 1880 publication were especially illuminating:

There is probably no river, in these times of polluted streams and close preserves, offering such advantages to the Manchester anglers as the Derbyshire Wye. This lovely water, and the vale

*through which it flows, are indeed difficult to surpass. Salmon
fishing has its triumphs, and to wave the hand o'er some northern stream, capturing the speckled beauties in Nature's wilds
and breathing the invigorating air of the moorland and mountain is also glorious; but these are more difficult to obtain. On
this water both the possession and opportunity are within the
reach of us all . . . the whole of these waters are fishable if a
ticket be obtained either at Rowsley's famous old inn, The
Peacock, or at the sign of the Rutland Arms at Bakewell.*

I re-read these words on the train between Derby and
Matlock, and learnt an important lesson about travelling
in the footsteps of the Victorian angler - their journeys
occurred in a specific industrial and economic climate,
when pollution and rapid population expansion forced
fishermen to venture further afield; the gap between the
rural idyll and the urban conurbations was widening. It
was railways which transformed an industrial revolution
in to a social one, and the fishermen of the northern
towns who journeyed to Bakewell and Rowsley did so
not simply to indulge a spirit of adventure, but also to
escape smoke-belching factories and claustrophobic cot-
ton mills, and to find peace in a new world. Much has
changed in one hundred years. The dark satanic mills are
now museums or waterfront apartments, class divides have
been disassembled and rebuilt in subtler ways and twenty-
first society has found other ways to screw itself up.
Before I'd even thrown a line, it was clear that I was not
casting in to the same waters as the men I was following.
   It was comforting to know that both the Peacock
Hotel and the Rutland Arms have survived in to the
twenty-first century when so much else from the era that

created them has been lost – and though the clientele are far more likely now to be tourists visiting Chatsworth House or Haddon Hall, a welcome can still be found for the visiting angler. In David Reid's time, Rowsley South Station would have been a bustling terminus, and would also have been the final destination for Manchester's fishermen (and, doubtless, others from Sheffield, Chesterfield and elsewhere) in search of Wye trout. Now, its use is reserved for the steam service I failed so miserably to take, but efforts are in hand to restore the line beyond Rowsley. The scheme has met with strong opposition from locals, who seemingly prefer the thunderous intrusion of the A6 along much of the river, and the outcome is far from certain.

Current objections are entirely in keeping with the Peak District's past. The railways there caused controversy from their inception. The new Midlands railway passed over the Wye after the opening of the Monsal Viaduct in 1863, and met with indignation from many who felt the beauty of the district had been destroyed; this particularly outraged John Ruskin – never a man to keep an opinion to himself – who lamented a godless world where trains could convey 'every Buxton fool to Bakewell in half an hour'. Ruskin had much to say during his long life on politics, religion, philosophy and his annulled, sexless marriage to Effie Gray, but his thoughts on Manchester anglers escaping the slums for a day went unrecorded.

There's something quite reassuring about the fact that a visit to the Peacock Hotel stretch of the Wye can still, as in the 1800s, be had for the price of a day ticket, and that any fool – from Buxton or even Swindon – can arrive by steam train if he so wishes.

The water available to us that afternoon amounted to three furlongs of wonderful trout stream. The river here passes through meadows and gentle hills, and its limestone waters run clear, thick with weed and insect life. Richard, a regular rod there, walked us along the beat, pointing out likely lies and the scenes of past triumphs and calamities. Everywhere, the river keeper's efforts to maintain a rich habitat for trout and other creatures were apparent. Large numbers of wild fish rose in the clear, ranunculus-rich water; the air fizzed with blue-winged olives, green drakes and a few black gnats. I didn't think we could fail to catch trout.

Richard advised that we tackle up long leaders - 12-foot or more - with 5lb points. It was up to us whether we chose to match the olives or the drakes. The riffles that were a feature of every pool would make drag a problem, but Richard assured me that a good cast and mend stood a chance of receiving some attention. My first cast fell short, but my second and third both elicited confident takes.

I missed both, but wasn't surprised. The first few trout of the new season always catch me off-guard after a languid winter of pike fishing. Richard and Yorkie, who had yet to tackle up, were highly amused. They were in no rush, having fished here many times before, and stood back testing their hook points, tugging at leader knots and drinking tea while I thrashed the first pool to foam.

Missed takes became a feature of the day; these were canny, educated trout. In 1882, Manchester angler George Sumner described the Rowsley trout as *'thoroughly acquainted with the curious vagaries of an artificial fly'*. Old George was right, and it became clear that our trout were every bit as fickle as his. The Wye is fished most days throughout the season, and these fish showed no interest in poor casts or injudicious fly selections. They showed a particular disdain for my regulation river flies – which had cost a more than reasonable sum from a fancy trout boutique – and much preferred Richard's self-tied variants. And so, Yorkie and I used these.

That said, we were on a well-populated trout stream towards the end of May, with two hatches occurring simultaneously. We caught trout. Richard landed the first, and biggest, on a modified Kite's Imperial. It was a heavily-spotted brown with distinctive coral edged fins and bright red spots towards its tail. We didn't weigh it, but it was probably over two pounds.

Soon afterwards, I lost one and landed my first. It was a rainbow, perhaps half the size of Richard's brownie, and resembled nothing I'd ever caught from stocked still-waters. The depth of its colours, the larger fully-formed fins, the wily aggression and wild demeanour all impressed. I wanted another, and shortly afterwards I caught one. Yorkie was downstream and out-of-sight, but I could hear splashes and chuckling and knew he was also having fun.

In the final hour I managed to hook and hang on to one of the brown trout, using Richard's cane rod. I had been using a carbon 5-weight, and it took ten casts and two pools to adapt to the slower rhythms of Tonkin bamboo. We had moved downstream to a sharp bend where the river narrowed beneath a canopy of trees. The third pool allowed only a short drift before whipping the fly under the bank, but an exquisite fish sat inches below the surface in the centre of the pool supping mayflies.

On the second cast it took my green drake – or rather Richard's cunning variant – swallowing it confidently in a momentary whirlpool, and zipping upstream and down for a minute before surrendering to the net. We admired it briefly in the fading light, marvelling once more at the red spots and coral-tipped fins. When I slipped it gently back in to the deep margins, the clear water looked black.

The urge to stay longer was overwhelming, but we had a schedule of sorts to keep to. I wanted to sleep where I fell and continue casting at sunrise, but the rigidity of pre-booked tickets and inflexibility of the post-Beeching network prevented such spontaneity. There was a very late supper waiting in Shropshire, and we were every bit as hungry as the fish. The three of us walked back to the main road, and – for the first time – began to think about the next journey. The morning train would take us west, to a flooded valley, more trout and a water full of ghosts.

The Peacock · Rowsley · Derbyshire

Chapter II

Vyrnwy

The magnificent trout of the Derbyshire Wye and the
intimacy of the river itself could have held my attention
for many days, and I had seen more than enough to
understand its appeal to the anglers of Manchester's
Victorian past, but there was a train to catch before my
waders had dried on that first day. We were abandoning
its fickle fish and complex hatches for an altogether different trout fishing experience. Our next stop was
Llanwddyn.

There are two Llanwddyns but only one appears on any
map. It is a small settlement in a valley beneath the
Berwyn Mountains in North Wales and has been there for
a little over a century. Llanwddyn boasts a community
hall, a post office - Mondays and Thursdays only - local
businesses offering camping and outdoor activities, and a
football team occupying a comfortable mid-table place
in the JT Hughes Montgomeryshire Mitsubishi League,
Division 2. It is the kind of quiet Welsh village you could
pass without noticing, unless you knew differently.

The other Llanwddyn is found a mile further up the same valley and is a ghost village, submerged by Victorian engineers in the 1880s beneath a new reservoir which would supply fresh water for the crowded slums of Liverpool. This act of ruthless pragmatism outraged the sheep farmers who were forced from their homes, but led to the creation of Lake Vyrnwy. With typical resourcefulness, the opportunity to develop a first-rate fishery and holiday destination was taken, and before the nineteenth century was over an excursion to the trout of Vyrnwy had become an essential date in the travelling angler's calendar.

It was on mine too - the prospect of a few trout, lunch in a Victorian sportsman's hotel and possible encounters with the ghosts of old Llanwddyn was too good to miss.

In my 1930s copy of *The Field's* *Where to Fish*, an entry for the Lake Vyrnwy Hotel (telephone number Llanwddyn 2) offered lake and river fishing, rough shooting, riding and tennis. It boasted that the lake was 'stocked annually with fish and food', helpfully pointing out that the nearest GWR stations were at Pen-y-bont-fawr (8 miles) or Llanfyllin (10 miles), and served by Oswestry and Gobowen. Other adverts from the late 1800s and early 1900s point out that visiting sports could be collected by horse-drawn carriage from the station, but such sublime luxury died with the arrival of the motor car.

On a wet May morning, Yorkie and I abandoned the train at Welshpool - Llanfyllin, like so many rural stations across Britain, was closed in the mid-Sixties on the orders of Richard Beeching - and loaded our fly rods in to a compact Fiat 4x4.

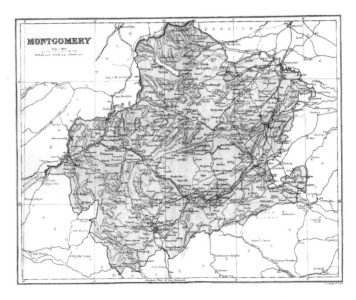

Map of Montgomery, showing lake Vyrnwy, Llanfyllin and Pen-y-bont-fawr stations.

I had read a little of Vyrnwy's history on the train. Liverpool's relentless expansion during the industrial revolution, and demands for clean water in an age of typhoid and cholera, made the construction of such a lake a necessity. The Berwyn Mountains through which the infant river Vyrnwy runs were chosen, not least because of their height above sea level and reputation for clear mountain stream water, and construction of the stone dam began in 1881. It took eight years and £620,000 to complete, and was a marvel of civil engineering at a time when similar projects were usually constructed from earth. A pointed gothic tower was erected thirty metres from the shore close to the hotel at the same time as the dam, giving one corner of the lake the appearance of a Bavarian idyll.

Above: Llanwddyn before the valley was flooded.

Right: Advert for Vyrnwy from the Fishing Gazette.

Below: The completed dam.

LAKE VYRNWY
NORTH WALES
EXCELLENT TROUT FISHING

Hotel stands 100 feet above lake, with magnificent views of mountains and moors. Lake 900 feet above sea level, five miles long. Fishing on lake and streams; also on 4½ miles Vyrnwy River. Recently re-decorated, good cuisine and cellar. Home farm produce. Post and telegraph office. Rough shooting.

TARIFF ON APPLICATION TO

MANAGER, LAKE VYRNWY HOTEL
OSWESTRY, NORTH WALES

Of course, beneath all this was old Llanwddyn. Before the valley flooded, engineers had razed the village to its foundations; the parish church, two chapels, ten farmhouses and thirty-seven smaller dwellings were demolished and rebuilt further down the valley. Eunant Hall, the manor house served by the local community, was knocked down but never replaced. Three inns and a post office were relocated, and even the village's dead were exhumed and reburied. In low water, foundations and roads can still be seen on the lake bed, and at such times it is comforting to know that the cadavers of ancient sheep farmers were not left behind.

It almost goes withot saying that this part of Wales is rich in folklore and myth, and barely a hill or valley exists without a gnome, troll or giant lurking in its past. One version of the Arthurian legend of Excalibur originated a few miles over the mountains in Snowdonia, while dragons are said to have once roamed freely in the region. Even the construction of the dam and lake at Llanwyddn added to the collective mythology. Before the valley could be flooded, a large rock called Careg Yr Yspryd (the ghost stone) had to be removed. This caused some consternation among locals, who knew that a legendary hero of the valley - the improbably named Dic Spot - had once trapped a mischievous goblin in the quill of a pen and placed it beneath the stone.

I was to learn later, in the bar of the hotel, that the ghost stone had been dynamited in 1887 and a large toad had crawled from the rubble. Neither the pen nor the goblin was found, and my informant suggested that both were still in the deep water by the lake's tower. He may have been right, but he was plastered and I suspected that this was a yarn he had spun a few times before. Certainly, none of the enquiries I had received to my weighted Gold-ribbed Hare's Ear that afternoon had even a hint of goblin about them.

Before fishing, Yorkie and I walked the full length of the dam - a little shy of four hundred metres in length and thirty metres thick - spotting the occasional rises and vortices of feeding trout. It was overcast and drizzling and I was keen to cast out, but my friend insisted that we spend an hour in the hotel first. I succumbed.

The hotel has managed the fishing on the lake, as well as some of the thirty-one rivers and streams running in to it, for over one hundred years. My trusted *Where to Fish* had the following to say in the late 1930s:

Vyrnwy; trout very numerous. Free risers, but small. Hotel very comfortable, excellent trout fishing. 14 boats and ghillies available, lake stocked annually. Tackle available from hotel. Illustrated booklet giving full particulars of fishing &c., may be had post free on application to the proprietor of hotel.

I had acquired another source of invaluable, if outdated, information prior to the trip. Richard Threlfall's *Notes on Trout Fishing on Lake Vyrnwy and the Upper Vyrnwy River* is a rare little book, published in 1947 in a limited run of five hundred and originally sold through the hotel. Serendipity - and an indecent amount of money for a book of only thirty-one pages - had brought it my way. Threlfall's intended readers were novice visitors to Vyrnwy, and sixty years notwithstanding, his book would prove a reliable reference for us both. Threlfall recommended only one dry fly - the beetle bug or *coch-*

Travelling from Llanfyllin station to the hotel used to be done in style!

y-bonddhu – and identified the two large bays at the head of the lake, Rhiwargor and Eunant, as the best places to start. He was dismissive, though, of some of the methods used in the 1940s:

The beetle brings the fish up all right, in fact the best fishing of the year may be expected when the 'cochy' is most plentiful. Some people fish for them with imitations made from cork, painted and varnished. These are difficult to throw any distance nicely and lightly, and one favourite method of fishing them, by letting them drift in the hope that a fish will some day see them, is dull beyond words.

Threlfall wrote his guide at the end of the war, and this is reflected in the prose; there are no goblins or Celtic heroes, no swords or ghostly stones. He wrote sparingly in austere times, and reference is made to local shortages, a 'make do and mend' attitude to tackle and the need to fish for the pot. Occasionally, he reminisces about the better sport and fine company of old. Even in 1947, the trout were getting smaller and the fishing more proletarian.

That said, a flavour of Victorian grandeur survives in the hotel, and this is reflected in both the décor and the prices. Yorkie and I enjoyed coffee on the veranda overlooking the lake, and were able to examine the hotel's fishing records, assiduously-documented in bound leather volumes. It seemed that we were just in time for the best of the sport. The most impressive entry we found was of a record fifty-nine-fish catch by Mr Morgan and Mr Everett in April 1912, but there were countless other days in April and May when trout appeared to lose all caution.

Yorkie and I discussed emulating this, and perhaps recreating one of those Edwardian photographs where two heavily-tweeded gents pose in front of obscene numbers of very dead trout, but quickly dismissed the idea - we were not in britches, neither of us could boast the obligatory handlebar moustache and it was already two-o-clock, which is far too late to begin a historic catch. Edwardian bounty hunters don't arrive in low emission Fiats either.

The original stock which entered the lake in 1888 was made up of Loch Leven browns, but twenty-first century sensibilities dictate that browns are out-numbered by the larger (and more easily-procured) rainbows, and it was these, the manager assured us, that would provide us with excellent sport. We were advised to tackle up with strong leaders. The chap selling the tickets always says something like that, but it was good to hear it all the same. Fishing days should begin with thoughts of monsters, even if they don't end that way.

The old fishing writers - with the exception of One-fly Threlfall - advised visiting sports to fill their japanned fly boxes with February Reds, March Browns, Green and Teals, Claret and Mallards and Wickhams, dressed small on 0 to 000 hooks, but the hotel manager had been less specific. "Use a nymph just below the surface and follow the wind," he had said.

He was more effusive on the subject of recent developments around the estate, and told us of the cyclists, walkers, climbers and horse riders who visited, of the Vyrnwy half marathon and the new sculpture trail that greeted the turn of the millennium below the dam. We learnt of the RSPB's hides around the lake and the ninety species of breeding birds in the area, which has long been afforded Nature Reserve and Conservation Area status. I couldn't fail to be impressed that this huge Victorian folly had, in the long term, done little to damage the region's ecology.

Yorkie and I had not been big-water trout fishing in recent years, but remembered the drill. I opted for an intermediate line with a variety of nymphs, my pal fished his with a long leader and floating line. We scouted the reedy top end of the lake in Boat 9, exploring the margins with Gold-ribbed Hare's Ears, Pheasant Tails and weighted Olives. The mountains hung over us, clad in thick heather and rough acidic grassland. An electric outboard propelled us silently across the water, and when we cut the engine the boat drifted gently with the prevailing current towards the dam. There was no discernible hatch taking place and few trout rose. The earlier wind had abated and so the surface was flat calm for much of the afternoon. When a slight breeze appeared, so did the fish, and we both caught rainbows approaching two pounds.

Both of us managed to lose fish too; mine were stockie rainbows of the same stamp as the fish we had in the boat, but Yorkie hooked a more substantial creature casting close to overhanging branches on the southern bank. It was there for a matter of seconds before rolling over the leader and throwing the hook, leaving only a swirling vortex and the briefest flash of a long and very deep silver flank.

We both cried out the customary expletive, and there followed a long silence before we continued fishing. Yorkie later claimed it had been the largest trout he'd ever hooked, and I believed him.

The light went within an hour and we reeled in. With the boat safely stored there was little to do but enlist the help of two other fishers in pushing the axle-deep Fiat up a waterlogged hill to the main road, and return to the hotel. Yorkie would go back to Shropshire in the morning and my rail-bound odyssey would continue without him. My next stops would be Gobowen, Shrewsbury and Newport, and I would finally disembark at Chippenham in time for Duffer's Fortnight on the Bristol Avon. There were six inconvenient weeks of teaching to endure, after which my longer journeys could continue.

But for now we were in Wales, drinking beer on a hotel veranda. Early starts and crowded platforms and hatches of mayflies could wait; a thousand acres of

Victorian endeavour stretched out below us, and it was an evening to toast our successes and remember the big one that had got away. As the night consumed the Berwyn Mountains the lost fish grew in our memories, and soon became the largest rainbow trout either of us could imagine. A second and third beer softened our disappointment, but not entirely. Somewhere out there an enormous trout, a mischievous goblin and the heroic Dic Spot were relishing freedom among the submerged streets of old Llanwddyn.

The post office at old Llanwddyn.

Chapter III

Shark Fishing in Looe

When the itinerary for these journeys was first drawn up, the proposed shark expedition to Looe was the one that excited me - and, if I'm honest, worried me - the most. It was certainly the one that took me furthest away from my comfortable angling world of secluded pools and vibrant rivers, to an altogether bloodier place inhabited by slightly-crazed men. It also necessitated stepping on to a boat, and being thrown around the waters of the Channel, some twenty-five miles from shore. That concerned me - my track record with boat fishing is less than auspicious. There was an ill-fated barracuda incident off Florida in 1981, and a channel wreck debacle in 1990, and both were blighted with vomiting to a degree not seen since Linda Blair's performance in *The Exorcist*. Since then, my fishing has been confined to land, calm Scottish lochs and the occasional Thames punt.

In short, I don't do boats. They don't like me, and I'm not overly fond of them.

So, days before my departure to Looe I stood patiently

in a queue at the Swindon branch of Boots hoping that the assistant would reach for some magic beans that could guarantee a settled stomach and flat calm seas. I came away with two wrist bands that promised to exert mystical pressure on my yin and yang, and a packet of travel pills with a reassuring picture of a boat - albeit a cross-channel ferry - on the front. They came with a warning about possible drowsiness. If these worked, and I was sceptical, it could be a life-changing event. I could finally, after forty years, become a boat angler. My smiling assistant had also suggested that I avoid alcohol and rich food for twenty-four hours before the trip - this too would necessitate a new life choice. I accepted the assistant's advice in good faith, and promised myself I would adhere to it. I really did.

Shark anglers, and particularly shark skippers, are a bit different to the rest of us. The sport itself bears so little resemblance to most forms of angling, and to my mind it has wildness and brutality that cannot be found else-where within fishing. When a Cornish adventure in search of them was first proposed, I was ready - if I came through it unscathed - to abandon roach and dainty floats and a car with a perpetual smell of trout pellets, and throw myself towards this new dangerous world. I told friends in the pub that I almost hoped one would give me a bite on the leg - nothing serious, but enough to leave a scar - and that I would then get the date and the weight of the fish tattooed beneath it.

Like most children, I was fascinated by the creatures themselves. I watched them on television, impersonated them when fooling around with friends in the Fareham Leisure Centre swimming pool and kept my Action Man

Diver 'with realistic rubber shark' far longer than could be considered reasonable for a growing lad. On family outings to Lee-on-Solent, my brother and I longed to see a deathly grey dorsal fin appear amidst screams and panic and a frenzy of running women in bikinis. It never happened, but like all boys in the 1970s, we were unable to be in or near the sea without subconsciously humming the *Jaws* theme. Sharks, like football and plastic dinosaurs and girls who won't talk to you, belong in every boy's life.

A fascination with sharks continued in to adulthood, but I never felt a desire to go and catch one. Tench, carp, pike, barbel, bass, trout and the occasional flounder were enough to be going on with - as were women in bikinis. Sharks belonged in Jacques Cousteau films, not on the end of my line. I admired them, and the strange weather-beaten men who pursued them, from a distance.

Perhaps the greatest shark hunter of them all was the quirky Montauk New Yorker Frank Mundus. Born in New Jersey in 1925, Mundus owned his first boat at the age of twenty-six, and quickly courted dockside controversy by towing a whale he had killed back to port. Unrepentant, he continued to use chopped whale in his rubby-dubby, and became locally famous for his deftness with a harpoon. In 1964, Mundus landed a 4,500lb Great White, and this did much to enhance his 'Monster Hunting' shark guide business. One of his customers in the Sixties was Peter Benchley, later the author of *Jaws*, and Mundus frequently claimed to be the inspiration behind the Captain Quint character. Benchley denied this, but there can be little doubt that the irascible

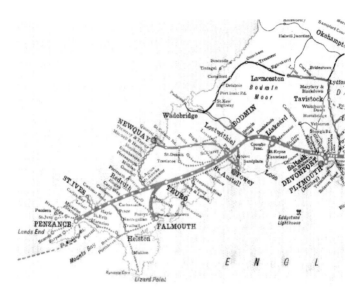

*1925 Great Western Railways map of the South West, showing the branch line to Looe.
The map below shows how the railways look today.*

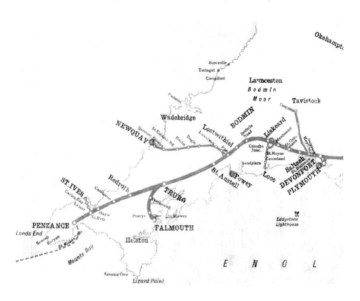

Mundus played up to the image, wearing a shark-tooth necklace and hooped earring, and painting his toenails red and green (to represent port and starboard, apparently). Mundus gave up sharking in the 1990s when the US Coastguard introduced a compulsory written exam for skippers, and ran a lemon farm with his wife through his retirement. Mundus' fame in later life was such that he appeared on both David Letterman's and Larry King's talk shows and his memoirs were published to much acclaim, with the memorable title *Fifty Years A Hooker*.

I watched Mundus being interviewed on an American cable channel during an otherwise dull evening in a Georgia motel room in the late Nineties. I don't remember what the programme was, but do recall thinking that all shark skippers had to have a little bit of Quint in them, and possibly a streak of madness. I still think so.

Looe might not have the cosmopolitan chutzpah of New York, and Sinatra almost certainly never sang about it, but it has long had shark, and its angling history is a colourful one. The 1925 edition of Great Western Railway's *Around the Coast with Rod and Line* has the following to say:

East and West Looe - famous angling resorts - and the nice little bay sheltered by St. George, or Looe, Island invite detailed description. Looe is one of Cornwall's fishing towns and formerly an important seaport. It is reached by rail from Liskeard in half an hour. The town occupies both banks of the Looe river, the western portion being the smaller and older. The little place boasts of a long history. In 1347 twenty ships and 315 marines were sent hence to the siege of Calais. In later years it was on several occasions subjected to the incursions of

Turkish and other pirates, and stories of the fights which ensued between the hardy Cornish sailors and the marauders are still told by their descendants.

The GWR guide suggests that Looe, in the inter-war years, was known for its pollack, bass, mackerel, whiting, sea bream, pouting and conger. No mention is made of shark, though we are told that London anglers frequently

The splendid Brigadier J. A. L. Caunter with his thresher shark of 268lb, caught in 1959.

journeyed by train to sample the pollack fishing in summer, and that Looe's famous 'banjo' pier was home, in winter, to 'very large Wrasse'. Much earlier, in the eighteenth century, drifting for pilchards was part of a vibrant local economy, alongside the export of copper from the docks.

The town's claim to be the home of English shark fishing dates back only to 1953, when the Shark Angling Club of Great Britain (SACGB) was founded there by Brigadier J. A. L. Caunter CBE MC. In 1959, a record blue shark of 218lb was caught from a Looe charter boat by a Mr Sutcliffe, and in 1971, a Mrs Yallops landed a 500lb mako from local waters. In his *Around the Coasts with Rod and Line*, Derek Fletcher, writing in 1960, wrote '*quickly to mind comes the name of Looe, where every year new headlines are made*'. Fletcher considered the local shark fishing in some detail:

Shark fishing will lure the big game angler and one needs to hire a suitable boat and skipper. Tackle is expensive to buy outright, but it can be hired and this is obviously the most sensible thing for holiday activities . . . Jack Bray, The Quay, East Looe, will be able to fix you up with shark trips and gear. He is the largest stockist of shark tackle in the British Isles and certainly a useful chap to know. Boats leave the quay daily from the beginning of June to mid-October and are at sea for about nine hours.

Commonest catch is the blue shark and there always seem to be plenty in season. They arrive in the Channel during May.

A cursory read of my dog-eared copy of Fletcher's book on the train from Liskeard revealed that, by the 1960s,

Looe had earned a nationwide reputation for its shark fishing; even in Fletcher's day, there were locals suggesting it had already become too commercialised and the fishing was in decline. This didn't surprise me; every prime fishing spot I have ever visited has its resident 'it ain't what it used to be' misanthropes. Catch returns maintained by the SACGB suggest that the detractors had a point. I just hoped that on this occasion, they were wrong.

Until recently, the club had met in what is now a pub called The Salutation, but it has recently moved to its own shore-front office. Business is brisk, albeit on a considerably smaller scale than in its heyday. Half a century ago, boats could be hired for £8, and a season's catches

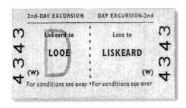

often numbered in excess of 3000 fish. Holidaymakers would wait for the evening to witness the catches being weighed on the quay, but modern sensibilities now dictate that specimens are measured and released. In 1958, the tally was a record 5,744. In the twenty-first century, there are fewer sharks, and fewer boats trying to catch them. A typical season sees two to three hundred blues caught between May and September.

Three hours on the First Great Western train out of Bath Spa took me as far as Liskeard. The train was unremarkable but comfortable, relatively quiet and we passed through exquisitely pastoral West Country scenery. I read a little, enjoyed a surprisingly good buffet coffee and relished my final unscarred hours on dry land. There had been no one at home to wave me off, no distraught girl worrying for my safety or promising to still love me if I returned with less limbs than expected, and the peacefulness of the Somerset and Dorset countryside further lessened my natural inclination towards melodrama. I was just going fishing, albeit for shark.

The regular service ended at Liskeard, and so I travelled on the little Looe Valley Line for the final few miles, dividing my time during this last half hour between Fletcher's book, staring out of the window at an increasingly watery landscape and translating the graffiti in my carriage. I vowed that if I could ever lay my hands on the principal artist - who had helpfully signed his work 'Dan da Man', or something similar, I really couldn't decipher it precisely - I would offer him to the local skippers for rubby-dubby.

Graffiti notwithstanding, the final miles of this journey are a delight. It is an old line; the original Liskeard and Looe Railway opened in December 1860, carrying granite from the mines on Bodmin Moor. The Liskeard to Looe Union Canal it replaced still runs alongside the track in places. A passenger service followed twenty years later, and when the GWR took over the route in 1909, Looe's promotion as a tourist location began. Until 1916 the line ended at the quay, but now it extends only to Looe station, overlooking the estuary where the East and West Looe rivers meet. The station itself belongs to another age. The single track, ending abruptly in buffers at the platform's end, the painted wooden structure and the refreshing lack of automated barriers evoke more innocent days, and the imagination could easily conjure up parting sweethearts, holidaying families without dysfunction and vicars on bicycles.

This magical piece of old England so nearly disappeared. In the mid-Sixties, the Looe Valley Line was identified as economically inefficient in Richard Beeching's *Reshaping of Britain's Railways* plan, and its closure was assured. Only two weeks before the agreed demise in 1966, the line received a reprieve from Minister for Transport, Barbara Castle. There is no evidence to suggest that Mrs Castle had the preservation of Looe's shark fishing reputation at the forefront of her mind, but this demonstration of faith has been rewarded;

annual passenger figures are rising, and now exceed 80,000.

From Liskeard, the train had passed through Coombe Junction Halt, St Keyne Wishing Well Halt, Causeland and Sandplace. The last mile of the journey ran alongside the estuary, and salt air had filled the carriage. I soon forgot about urban scrawl, the Beeching Report and extravagantly-coiffured socialists - the prospect of encountering a shark had become very real, and by the time we came to a gentle rest against the buffers, I had begun to feel a little apprehensive.

I had done a little research on blue sharks in the previous week, and had found them to be fascinating. Atlantic blues (*Prionace glauca*) migrate eastwards in the spring, riding the Gulf Stream, covering distances in excess of 3000km. Traditionally, they begin to appear in the channel around May, and mid-summer sees them present in English waters in greatest numbers. Most sources confirmed that they are generally lethargic but capable of great speed (second only to makos). More worryingly, the editor of an English surfing website had informed me that blues rank among the twenty species 'most likely to attack man, dude'. Blues are, I was told, prone to hunt in numbers, and have been found feeding in areas where air and shipping disasters have occurred.

That said, records of human fatality from attacks by blues are rare, and some researchers put the numbers of such incidents in single figures. I had no intention of adding to this. My surfing friend had dismissed my concerns - 'just stay in the damn boat, man'.

My hosts in Looe were Cornish Dave and his family. Dave lives in a charming Victorian house overlooking the harbour, and directly opposite the Shark Angling Club of Great Britain's HQ. We'd met once before, introduced by a mutual friend at a Southampton football match which had ended disastrously - Saints games often do. Perhaps to cancel out our inauspicious history, Dave marched me straight to a pub with offers of Cornish Beer. By the time we arrived at his house an hour later, we'd been in some other pubs, and I was closely acquainted with the local ale - Doom Bar and Tribute both proved particularly memorable. We were both a little shame-faced when Dave's wife reminded us that there was a barbeque to attend. More alcohol, and industrial quantities of rich food, followed. Still on dry land, my sea legs had already developed a distinct wobble. I imagined the Boots assistant tutting furiously, but she hadn't reckoned on the formidable allure of West Country hospitality.

The following morning, we met our skipper at Shark HQ. Mally Toms is one of eight skippers who run boats out of the harbour on behalf of the SACGB, and his credentials are second to none. He told me that he'd been fishing these waters for over forty years, and it would be fair to say he has the leather-skinned no-nonsense shark hunter demeanour and 'there be monsters out there' patter down to a tee. Throughout our long day, he never did spit tobacco towards the horizon or utter the immortal line 'I think we're going to need a bigger boat', but it felt like he might at any moment.

We left Looe harbour at 9am in *Jo-Dan*, a 33-foot Reliant, and a two hour journey in to the deep water twenty-five miles from shore followed. At anchor, the first job was to catch some mackerel, and these were as obliging as ever. There were five anglers aboard - Dave, his son Chris, a chap whose name never emerged but who Mally cruelly christened Quasimodo, and a long-time shark man named Tom, who bore the scars of more than a few battles and said little, preferring to sit silently in the cabin's canopy protected from the elements by a thin bomber-jacket of Seventies vintage.

Mally set up five shark rods in the 50-80lb class, each with large floats and 12 foot wire traces. Tom, a veteran of this sort of thing, arranged the drawing of lots, and we were allocated a rod each. By this point, I should add, I had thrown up the morning's scrambled eggs, and much of the previous day's feast, but was feeling relatively good. Chris, a history student more at home in the sedate but equally ruthless world of big money poker than the blood-and-vomit reality of a shark boat, was suffering similarly. Dave was bounding round the boat like he'd done it all his life, and Quasi and Tom were similarly nonchalant, though the former warned me that - in spite of his years working on tugs - he was highly likely to join the ranks of the infirm once the drift began. It was, Mally assured us, a simple Force 4 to 5, and we should expect action imminently.

Imminence, in shark fishing terms, can mean anything. On that day, it meant four hours of inactivity (if the occasional bout of mal-de-mer is conveniently forgotten). Time passed slowly, with *Jo-Dan* drifting on an increasingly angry tide. Chris and I steadfastly kept our eyes fixed on the horizon, declining food and beer. Tom sat silently in the cabin's porch, as the rain increased. Mally talked, constantly - he spoke of sharks caught and lost, monsters every one of them, and lamented the declining numbers of fish. The rods were motionless, their multiplier reels silent. Occasionally, one outfit would be reeled in to check the mackerel flappers or adjust the depth of the float, and these tasks invariably fell to Mally. In a shark boat of this sort, the Skipper does it all, and the anglers are redundant until the sharks arrive.

In the final hour, Dave's rod (number five in Tom's lottery) bucked violently as something peeled a frightening length of line off the old Penn reel in a matter of seconds.

"Shark!" shouted Mally.

I swore, loudly, though I can't be sure why. Chris turned a little paler, Quasi and Tom stepped back to watch the drama unfold and Mally jumped to Dave's side to offer instruction. This was Dave's first shark, and the next twenty minutes were a tense affair. The reel was an ancient one, and the clutch a little sticky. Dave slackened it off, then tightened it, and on both occasions was told by our skipper in brutally Anglo-Saxon terms not to mess about with it. After three thumping dives to the sea-bed, the shark managed to wrap itself in the trace, and Dave was able to pump it to the surface. The first flash of electric blue in the water, twenty feet down, confirmed our suspicions - Dave was attached to a bluey, and a pretty big one too. Mally donned his gloves, grabbed trace and fish, and seconds later the creature joined us in the boat.

I'd not seen a shark in a boat before, and claim no expertise, but this was one was unequivocally fed up about being there, spitting the hook out and sabotaging our efforts to photograph it, measure it, tag it and release it. I was surprised at my courage during the process. At one point, I was almost within ten feet of the fish.

Within a minute or two we had established that Dave's fish was a little over seven feet in length (and therefore big enough to secure him membership of the SACGB), and it was spiralling back in to the depths, more or less unscathed. Dave was delighted, and the collective spirit on the boat was joyous. Just seeing one of these remarkable creatures was special, and the identity of the captor almost irrelevant.

At least, that is what four of us told ourselves. Dave just grinned.

Mally was sure we might get another chance, but silence returned and it was soon time to return to shore. The journey back was quicker, a little over an hour-and-a-half, and we arrived in Looe with the red and white shark flag flying. A quick survey of the other boats revealed that ours was the only fish of the day. I'd turned from green to a reasonably healthy pink, and even Chris had regained his usual pallor. A large cigar was lit, and the wrist bands discarded. My yin and yang had let me down miserably, and the predicted drowsiness had been a chore, but the joy of seeing Dave's big blue, and the knowledge that its capture necessitated more Cornish beer that night, was ample compensation.

I left for Looe station the following morning, walking down the estuary wall and over the seven arches of the nineteenth-century road bridge. The skippers were busily preparing their boats for a new day's adventures, but the urge to join them had gone. I stopped to say farewell to Mally, and he told me - with more than a glimmer of mischief in his eyes - that there was one place left on *Jo-Dan* that day. I politely declined, having accepted overnight that my sea legs were insufficient for this sort of thing, and sharks were best left to hardier sorts - men like Mally Toms, Frank Mundus and Cornish Dave.

I returned to Wiltshire a little chastened, now confirmed as a land-based angler with two unmolested legs and no new tattoos to show in the pub. On the train back to Bath Spa, I thought about roach and floats, and the sweet smell of trout pellets in the boot of the Peugeot.

A month later, I read of Frank Mundus's death in Hawaii, at the age of eighty-two. The obituaries were colourful, and kind. He had spent one final summer in Montauk, and suffered a fatal heart attack on the last day. The real Captain Quint was dead, but my brief visit to Looe had taught me that wherever there are sharks, there will be weather-beaten old sea dogs taking to the waters and pursuing them, with cold steely eyes and just a little streak of madness.

Chapter IV

Along the Thames

The river Ray runs through the grounds of the large secondary school where I teach in Swindon. It is an unremarkable stream, filled with the inevitable shopping trolleys and discarded syringes that blight so many urban waterways, but it does hold a few stunted chub which amuse the young anglers of Moredon and Pinehurst. Downstream, it meanders through park land and housing estates, and eventually joins the Thames. I have never fished the Ray, though I drive over it twice a day and hear about its captured inhabitants from pupils every Monday morning. What does please me, however, is the thought that the trickle outside my classroom window is umbilically connected to the greatest fishing river of them all. The molecules that I and a few bored teenagers gaze at on listless afternoons eventually find their way to the mother water, through the meadows of Castle Eaton and Hannington and onwards to great angling stations like Marlow, Kingston and Richmond.

Nobody eats the fish from the Ray - not even the

more cavalier Year Nine boys - and doing so would test the boundaries of both legality and common decency, but further downstream it was once a different tale. Until the 1850s the fish of the Thames were plundered by the men from Billingsgate and sold to scrofulous Londoners who could afford no better and were grateful for whatever polluted offerings they could obtain. Allegedly, the Jewish community were particularly fond of the barbel, though others named them 'mud vermin'. The arrival of refrigeration and the rail network in the nineteenth-century made the netting of freshwater fish unnecessary, and England's palate became altogether saltier in subsequent years. The bream and pike no longer worried about nets and boatmen. Instead, they faced an onslaught from a new breed of travelling angler who could reach any munificent spot within hours.

Before Victoria's century was over, the railway companies had established a complex range of Anglers' Privilege Tickets. They worked alongside some of the finest angling administrators - men like Philip Geen and Thomas Spreckley - and ensured that fishermen along the Thames could travel the railways for a preferential rate on production of their T.A.P.S (Thames Angling Preservation Society) or London A.A. club card. Weekend mornings saw anglers in their hundreds shouldering their creels at the capital's stations and setting out for a day on the river. Such was the fame of the anglers' trains that writers like Arthur Smith (author of *The Thames Angler*) were driven to some highly questionable verse.

Oh! I am a jolly passenger, and love the second class,
I sigh not for the covered seats, I am not such an ass;

To Richmond eighteen pence I pay, and first class cars I hate,
They charge a shilling more each way, and won't a farthing
  bate.
We're in the second class, ha! ha! We're in the second class.
My rod and basket's on the seat, I've nothing else besides,
Except my baits, and those I keep along with me to ride.
And should a sudden storm come on, as down the line we
  speed,
I mock its anger, cos I know it puts roach on the feed.
We're in the second class, ha! ha!
We're in the second class.

Railway company angling guides soon appeared, mercifully devoid of sub-musical hall doggerel, and championed the Thames from the mid-1800s until the 1930s. The GWR's *Haunts and Hints for Anglers* had the following to say:

Furnishing sport along its course for something like 130 miles, the Thames is undoubtedly the premier angling river of the British Isles for general fish. The Thames may be said to be open to the public along its entire length - a priceless boon to those who delight, spring, summer, autumn and winter to visit the charming districts through which it runs. The facilities for reaching the numerous fishing stations are at all times excellent. Indeed, the Great Western Railway might have been laid down to cater for Thames anglers, for they no sooner leave the train at some resorts than they are on the banks of their favourite river.

The GWR had a point. So many of the finest fishing spots - Reading, Windsor, Datchet, Staines, Penton Hook, Shepperton, Hampton Court, Molesey Weir,

G.W.R.

THE UPPER THAMES.

RETURN FARES BETWEEN PADDINGTON

AND			First			Third	
Abingdon*	...	...	17	10	...	10	2
Bourne End	...	...	7	0	...	3	6
Cookham	...	...	7	0	...	3	6
Culham*	...	...	16	4	...	9	4
Goring & Streatley	...		13	2	...	7	6
Henley-on-Thames	...		10	6	...	5	11
Maidenhead	...	...	7	0	...	3	6
Marlow	...	...	8	0	...	3	11
Oxford	...	...	18	6	...	10	7
Pangbourne	...	...	12	3	...	6	11
Reading	...	...	10	6	...	6	0
Shiplake	...	...	10	0	...	5	8
Staines	...	...	4	8	...	2	6
Taplow	...	...	6	6	...	3	6
Tilehurst	...	...	11	3	...	6	5
Twyford	...	...	9	0	...	5	2
Wallingford	...	...	15	0	...	8	6
Windsor & Eton	...		5	6	...	3	0

Tickets available by any train, and to return any day
within SIX MONTHS.
* Higher fares applicable viâ Oxford.

COMBINED RAIL and RIVER THAMES VALLEY CIRCULAR TOUR TICKETS

in connection with Messrs. Salter Bros.' Oxford and Kingston
Steamers, are issued *during the Summer Months* from

Abingdon	Cheltenham	Liverpool	Staines
Aylesbury	Chester	Maidenhead	Swindon
Banbury	Ealing	Manchester	Wallingford
Basingstoke	Goring and	Marlow	Westbourne Park
Bath	Streatley	Newbury	Windsor & Eton
Birkenhead	Henley-on-	Oxford	Wolverhampton
Birmingham	Thames	Paddington	Worcester
Bristol	High Wycombe	Pangbourne	
	Leamington	Reading	
	etc.	etc.	etc.

For further information, send postcard to Superintendent of the
Line, Paddington Station, W.

FRANK POTTER, *General Manager.*

Kingston and Teddington, to name just some - were only a few minutes' walk from the nearest station.

Fortunately, they still are, and the Thames angler can still travel along much of its length with little trouble. Sadly, the thriving angling industry has declined, not least because the fish have declined similarly. The era of the Thames Professional Fishermen, men like Walter Coster, Wormy Webb, Job Brain and Blower Brown, has passed, and with their passing has gone some of the river's most strident colour. The Thames Professionals were hard workers, often hard drinkers, sometimes luckless gamblers, and plied their trade with competitive fervour. *The Fishing Gazette* of the late 1800s frequently reported their misdemeanours, and the battles over reserved pitches (secured with a rye peck but often misappropriated by a rival) could occasionally result in riverside fist fights. Nevertheless, the professionals were guardians of a thriving river. Patrick Chalmers, perhaps the finest chronicler of the river's golden years, wrote:

Every riparian village had its professional fishermen . . . and each professional had a lucrative clientele, a waiting list perhaps, of what Mr James Englefield has called 'fortunate aspirants for Trouting and other Thames honours'. Men came to Thames in the London train full of cash and credulity.

The Victorian angler liked to drink, and was rarely far from temptation. The Railway Guides frequently referred to favoured watering holes and cosy overnight stops, and there were lots of them. Perhaps inevitably, the anglers' hotels and inns have now disappeared, or diversified to become restaurants and wine bars offering conferencing facilities, family dining or - in the case of one famous old fishing pub near Lechlade - steam rallies and weekly live jazz. Few of them welcome weary fishermen in damp trousers and wet wellies. Our modern Thames has a little more saxophone, but a bit less soul.

Soul or not, I rarely need much persuasion to visit the river, and when this book's premise was first conceived a trip was hastily pencilled in to the itinerary. The Thames is a diverse river, however, and a solitary visit was never going to suffice. It is a summer barbel river, with extensive shallows and streamer weed, but it is also a winter river, deep and frigid and home to large pike. There are large shoals of perch, bream too, which can be caught throughout the year, and little-known colonies of enormous carp. A man could spend a lifetime on Old Father, but there were other journeys to make and so I went three times.

The first journey took me as far as Marlow, via Reading and Maidenhead, on a cloudless June morning. I travelled on the early First Western service, jostling with commuters who glanced suspiciously at my canvas rod bag, army surplus rucksack and frankly dishevelled condition. They all wore a look of urgency, and carried the disapproving air of people who are off to spend a day staring at screens or attending meetings, knowing that the scruffy ne'er-do-well sharing their carriage will be sat by a river contributing precisely nothing to the nation's GDP. They had important things to do, money to make and a profit war to fight, and I was simply having fun. In different times, they might have handed me a white feather.

I had, by now, become accustomed to this; in Geen's

*Left: Fishermen's retreats
along the Thames and
(below) the incredibly
handy* Oarsman's And
Angler's Map of the
Thames, *first published
by James Reynolds &
Sons in 1881. The map
unfolds to nearly nine
feet long!*

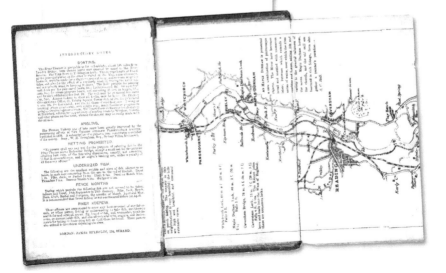

time, the angler would have been a familiar site on the nation's platforms. In the twenty-first century we are an oddity, an anachronism even, and bait-stained camou-flaged clothing does little to endear us to the inhabitants of a crowded carriage. Within minutes, a faint tang of trout pellets started to linger among capitalism's foot sol-diers.

By 9am I was in the lower car park of the Compleat Angler, shaking hands with my host, renowned river warden Roger Wyndham Barnes. Both are institutions and merit further description.

The hotel dates back to the days of Izaak Walton, and was originally a small hostelry with six rooms, owned by Wethereds Brewery and called the Riverside Inn. In the subsequent four centuries it has grown considerably, changing its name and passing through several owners including Alfred Yarrow of Yarrow's Shipyard and Lord and Lady Dawson; he was the king's physician and had little interest in running a pub and so, in the 1930s, it was passed to their daughter, Lady Bowater. Since 1980, it has succumbed to corporate ownership, but its reputation for excellent food and glorious setting hasn't diminished. The Compleat Angler has long held a reputation as a haunt of intellectuals, artists and royalty, too. Noel Coward, Tallulah Bankhead, J. M. Barrie, Dame Nellie Melba and Queen Elizabeth have all dined there. Of course, Roger and I had no intention of dining, and it is conceivable that we may not have satisfied the dress code anyway - our attention lay with the barbel, perch and chub that populate the weir pool below Tierney Clarke's magnificent suspension bridge.

Roger is Marlow's most arresting historical treasure.

This is how it should have looked - a dramatic arrival at Rowsley station aboard Peak Rails' WD150 Royal Pioneer - a proper, puffing train. Unfortunately, due to no fault of my own, I missed it . . .

Above: Fishing the Derbyshire Wye near the Peacock Hotel.

Below: The famous Peacock.

Right: Vyrnwy at its atmospheric best. Viewed from the Vyrnwy Hotel balcony.

Far left: Leaving Looe harbour for a day's sharking.

Left: Cornish Dave fighting his blue shark.

Below: Dave's blue comes alongside for tagging.

Above: Roger Barnes - the last of the Thames boatmen.

Below: A beautifully marked Thames pike.

Above: The Royal Scotsman carriage at Perth.
Below: The old station at Strathpepper.

Top: Casting in the wilds of Cape Wrath.

Above: A bit of a pollock . . .

Right: The old anglers' hotel at Cape Wrath.

For over twenty years, he has guided Thames fishermen on his two boats - *Muddy Waters* and *The Compleat Angler*. He sits comfortably in the tradition of the Thames Professionals and is deeply immersed in the river's history. When not rowing in the wake of Wormy Webb or Walter Coster, Roger is a writer, a connoisseur of unspeakably potent ale and a blues harmonica player and singer of ferocious intensity. Reviews have compared him, quite accurately, to Howling Wolf and Captain Beefheart. Neither the Wolf nor the Captain knew the first thing about barbel, though, and Roger most certainly does. Before our trip I had been told more than a few tales about him, and it was reassuring to discover that most were true.

From the first cast, we knew it would be a difficult day. The sky was cloudless, the temperature high, and the river clear. Beneath the froth and foam it was possible to peer in to eighteen feet of water and see a thick carpet of weed on the riverbed. A year before, clients had boated barbel to over twelve pounds, but there was little hope of casting in to a clear patch with the heavy leads required to hold bottom. Against Roger's better judgement I persevered with this for two hours, but every retrieve brought back a dense clump of greenery, and a great deal of cursing. It didn't help that Roger and I had both just given up smoking.

By mid-morning we were trotting maggots down a calm line on the far side of the pool. Bites were frequent, but bleak and tiny perch were our only reward and so we upped anchor to explore the river upstream. Roger took me to Temple Weir and Hurley Lock, and told me tales of the Viking long-boats arriving at Dane's Field. My host's eyes rarely left the water, but I detected more than a glint of wistfulness in them when he talked of ninth-century invaders and the panic their arrival would have caused amongst the riverside villagers. He was less effusive when we drifted past Bisham Abbey, frequented by David Beckham and his fellow England players in recent years prior to their (often disastrous) home internationals.

Today's bounty was not to be a net full of fish, but rather the chance to open a beer or two with Roger, drift aimlessly down the river and listen to an old Thamesman's tales. These were plentiful. I asked my boatman about his role as River Warden.

"The river warden job is entirely voluntary. I saw an advert that said 'river wardens wanted', and thought it sounded like a paying gig - it wasn't. The River Thames Society wanted people to watch over the river, keep an eye on it. I applied and they accepted me. The Society is a group of people who care passionately about the heritage and preservation of the river, and tend to oppose any obnoxious developments. They cover the river from Tideway to source, on the three parts of the Thames, the upper, middle and lower. We are expected to go on regular walks, write four reports a year and call in anything we see - dead fish, sunk boats, fallen trees, signs of pollution. I do less now that I have moved to Marlow as they already have a Warden here, but I still write for their magazine, the *Thames Guardian*. I'm sort of a Natural History correspondent. Recently I've written about the loss of Horse Chestnuts through disease and the Koi Herpes Virus that has arrived through the floods. I've done it for over ten years, but have worked on the river as a professional fisherman for longer.

"My daughter's mother was a teacher and earned more money than I did, so when she was born I suddenly became a house husband. I was doing odd gardening jobs, that sort of thing, and not bringing in very much. I spent a day fishing with a pal down near Henley and that evening we went to the Flower Pot for a pint. There was a sign on the wall there, barely legible now, which said something about 'Fishing and Boating Parties Catered For' - an old Edwardian sign it was. This was during Thatcher's Britain, and the era of corporate entertainment - Wimbledon, Test Cricket, golfing days and so on, and I thought that there would be people who would rather have a day fishing than golf. My friend offered to bankroll me a boat, and I could pay him back as and when - I only had an 8-foot dinghy then - and so I went to the Boat Show and bought one. I began advertising and, through word of mouth, it grew."

The sun put an end to all thoughts of fish in the mid-afternoon, so Roger told me of his hitch-hiking days, of eighteen months spent busking down Route 66 with a rucksack, guitar, harmonica and fishing rod for company. We slowly blistered in the heat and drifted downstream on ancient molecules, and Roger told me a memorably offensive joke that cannot be re-told here but kept me chuckling for hours. We agreed that it was a hopeless day for fishing, but a special one all the same.

As the sun finally came off the water we returned to Marlow Weir and tried once more for the barbel, but again the weed and sub-surface cabbages defeated us. The barbel were there, shoals of chub too, but penetrating the foliage to present a bait to them was seemingly impossible. At dusk, Roger made for shore, cryptically promising that I would see a monster barbel before the day was out.

He was right, too. With the boat stowed away for the night beneath a canopy of willows, the wily professional led the way down country lanes to the Lands End pub at Charvil. I'd not been there before, and Roger wasted no time in introducing me to the pub's most auspicious regular. Above the fireplace, preserved for forty years in an unremarkable bow-fronted case, sat Charlie Cassey's record-breaking barbel. It was a fish I'd written about in *A Can of Worms*, and I'd read the *Angling Times* account of its capture on Colonel Crow's water at Ibsley a dozen times or more, but this was our first encounter and I was captivated. It was ample compensation for the absence of barbel in our nets that day. Roger just grinned from behind his pint. The old bluesman had pulled it off again.

Two months later I returned to Marlow. Roger had called a week previously, telling me that the bigger perch were gathering in the slack water downstream by the Sea Scout Hut. He had also reminded me, with the gentle good manners of the finest Thames Professional, that I owed him money for the last trip, had promised to lend him my collection of Warren Zevon albums, and had admitted on our last excursion to having never landed a perch over a pound.

A skilled Professional with a knack for conjuring up big fish can get away with this sort of cheek towards a client, particularly when they are unequivocally correct on all counts, and so I packed my perch floats, a gallon of maggots and the collected recordings of Chicago's finest grunge-folk-pop troubadour in to the rucksack and returned to the Compleat Angler. This time, I took the mid-morning train, missing the commuters and instead sharing a carriage with two tie-dyed teenagers who, in an act of astonishing dexterity, were able to listen to their iPods and snog relentlessly from Reading to Maidenhead. The Bank Holiday weekend had just passed, and these two were, I guessed, returning home from the Reading Festival. They reeked of unwashed socks and home-grown dope, and reminded me of a former life when thoughts of big perch were less mesmerising. I was tempted to engage them in conversation, but neither came up for air.

Roger was right about the perch, but they ignored our maggots. In the Sea Scout Hut Bay, bleak were skittering and flashing on the surface as predators harried them from below, and so we resorted to fishing live baits under heavy bobs, drifting them towards the bank. Across the calm water of the bay, spiked dorsal fins occasionally broke surface and it became all too apparent that there were large shoals of these once rare fish swimming and feeding in front of us.

The recent perch renaissance is well-documented, but anglers of a particular vintage remember leaner times. When I was a boy fisher, perch had been decimated by disease and were as likely a prospect in my local waters as a coelacanth. I knew them from pictures in *Uncle Bill's Guide to Freshwater Fishing*, but was in my teens before I saw one over three ounces in weight. Now they are back, and reaching impressive sizes. We caught steadily, the fish averaging over a pound and peaking at a few ounces under three. These were big perch - not monsters by recent standards perhaps, but large enough.

Such days are rare, particularly on a river as mercurial

as the Thames, and thus worthy of celebration. Inevitably, Roger knew just the place. This time, he took me to the Flower Pot Hotel at Aston, near Henley, a watering hole famed equally for its food, beer and collection of taxidermy. We greatly enjoyed all three.

I was pleased to discover that the Flower Pot was still run by Brakspear's, who once employed the greatest of Thames trout fishers, A. E. Hobbs. Sadly, the pub's taxidermy didn't include Hobbs' own collection, much of which is currently gathering dust in a museum's storage rooms - to the eternal shame of those charged with celebrating the river's history. Nonetheless, the cased specimens at the Flower Pot were both fascinating and diverse. There were giant trout, of course, but goldfish, tench, gudgeon and an adult fox also jostled for space with the regulars.

Roger was kind enough to offer me his spare room that night, and I accepted. It turned in to the sort of evening that lucky anglers know only too well. Songs were sung, spirits consumed and stories retold. At some point I managed to drop his vintage Gibson acoustic guitar, but Roger was in benevolent mood. I crawled off to bed as the sun was rising, with blurred vision and Roger's cat, Whizzie, for company. When I woke, the house was empty; Roger, ever the professional, was out on the river with two clients. Wormy Webb would have been proud of him.

I gathered my rods and rucksack and walked to the station, knowing only too well that - once again - nobody would want to sit next to me on the journey home.

My final train-bound excursion took me higher up the river, to Culham. The village sits just downstream of

Abingdon, and a small club rents an ox-bow island below the weir. I'd fished there before, for barbel and the growing population of large escapee carp, but it was late October and the fields wore a morning frost. Lures, spinners and a bag of frozen herring sat in the bottom of the rucksack, beneath two flasks of soup and what passes for my wire trace box (a tobacco tin with a drawing of Frank Zappa on its battered lid). I was alone, and was after one of Old Father's legendary pike.

Culham has long had a reputation as a prime fishing station. Charles Dickens Junior described it in 1887 as '*a fine reach for pike*', while my dog-eared *Haunts and Hints* summarised it thus:

It is an ideal place for bank angling operations. It deserves to be fished much more than it is . . . experienced wielders of the rod speak highly of it. The stock of fish there is both varied and numerous. The railway station is close by, there is an express train service, and though fifty-six miles by rail from town the angler will have a good time for fishing even on the shortest of winter days.

The river was up and slightly coloured, but there was clear water in the margins and the banks were empty. The walk from the station had taken fifteen breathless minutes, and I was glad to flick a float-fished herring in to the weir pool and catch my breath. Nothing stirred below the surface, there or in any of the likely spots, and three hours passed without an enquiry. By then, I had fished the length of the club water and reached the free fishing stretch at the southernmost end, where canal boats and neglected cruisers were moored up for the winter.

My return ticket was for the evening commuter train, and so there was time to retread my morning route in reverse. By the time I arrived back at the weir pool in the final hour of light the pike had begun to feed. Two lively jacks of about five pounds first broke the silence but the third bite was slow, tentative and altogether different and I struck in to something immovable. The unseen cause was all weighty lethargy, and circled in the deep water below the lasher for ten minutes before rising. Her tail hung over the cord as she slid into the net.

It was almost time to leave, though it took a while to collect myself, and for my heart to adopt its usual rhythm. More of Arthur Smith's verse sprung to mind when I finally shouldered my creel and made for Culham station. It was a couplet from his *Angler's Alphabet*.

> *I was the Inn at the side of the river, where we all went to have our fish cooked.*
> *J was a jack, that greedy old liver, who fights precious hard when he's hooked.*

My last fish of the day had been neither a Jack nor a 'he', and had taken the spring balance to just under twenty pounds. She was not destined for the cooking pot of a riverside inn either, and was gently slipped back in to a pool below the weir instead. Her final defiant gesture had been a tail-spray of water and an angry boil of green and bronze and white.

The pike vanished to sulk somewhere deep and unseen, and Old Father flowed on - a hundred miles and more of molecules and history. I was soon on a train heading west, surrounded once again by commuters. They stared incredulously at the grinning camouflaged man who carried a faint smell of herring. I wanted to sing, but resisted the temptation to revive Arthur Smith's forgotten opus. They'd had a busy day, and wouldn't have understood.

THE THAMES AT RICHMOND.

Chapter V

The Grand Tour - Part I

During the long winter nights when seated around the fire, pipe well alight,
turning over the pages of some sporting book, the angler's thoughts instinctively
wander through the smoke far away in to the hills to his favourite holiday haunts
among the ancient bens and glens which he learned to love so well.
R. MacDonald Robertson - *Wade the River, Drift The Loch*

If one journey typified the travels of adventurous
Victorians, it was the grand tour of Scotland. These were
not the third-class day trips enjoyed by ordinary
Thamesmen, but extended excursions for the moneyed
gentleman hunter. Shotguns, servants and rod boxes with
Pall Mall addresses would be loaded on to the north-
bound trains, with stags and salmon waiting dutifully at
the end of the line.

That is how I have always imagined it, anyway, and
the literature of the late nineteenth and early-twentieth
centuries suggests there was some truth in this. The
writings of T. H. White, Frederick Aflalo, Captain Albert
F. L. Bacon and countless others record an age of endless
salmon and wild moors, peat-fired lodges and wisened
ghillies in kilts, and a world of rigid class distinction where

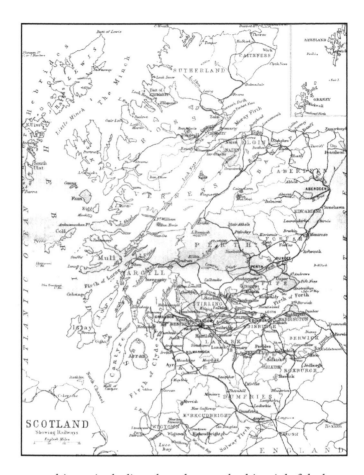

everything - including the salmon - had its rightful place. The Grand Tour was as much a part of a wealthy gentleman's life as his London club, his Alma Mater or his mistress.

Despite being deficient in all three, I decided to travel north nonetheless.

As soon as the planning began, I was reminded of a familiar truth; these journeys had been so much more straightforward in the days of steam. A century ago, seven different rail companies puffed and bellowed in to Scotland, and local branch lines often provided stations within walking distance of favoured salmon pools, lochs and lodges. For the Victorian angler with sufficient funds, it could be easy. Today, the Anglo-Scottish border is crossed only by the East and West Coast lines, and the network beyond Inverness is fragmented at best. Ticket prices can be outrageous for those who cannot book months in advance, and the reality is that it is cheaper to travel from England to France for its gigantic carp and catfish than it is to take a train to Scotland and try to search out one of its dwindling stocks of salmon.

Bloated Gallic cyprinids were not part of angling's golden age, however, and therefore have no place in this story, and so I booked a return ticket to Perth. I've long regarded this delightful town on the banks of the Tay as the gateway to the highlands, though locals would suggest the real mountains begin farther north, and it seemed as good a place as any to begin a Scottish adventure.

My plan from there was loose at best - it was the beginning of August, and I knew from previous experience that the grilse might just be running up the Cromarty Firth, past the Black Isle and in to the Averon. This, as always, would depend upon whether there was any water in the river, and I wouldn't know that until I got there. If the water was low and the salmon were in the estuary, there were trout in Sutherland that I knew I could catch, mackerel off the pier at Ullapool, a ferox-fishing ghillie on Loch Ness I had long wanted to meet and a deep limestone loch full of wild brownies and ghosts in the far north at Cape Wrath. My car was back in Wiltshire with a flat battery and perforated exhaust, and so the entire tour would rely upon trains, buses and the kindness of others. To complicate matters, Vic had decided to come with me to take photographs and see what all the fuss was about. We had two weeks in front of us, and only the vaguest of itineraries - up the East Coast and back down the West, with two travel rods and a rucksack full of flies and spinners. There would be no servants to carry the equipment, no loch-side stations and only an outside chance of a wisened old man in a kilt to net our fish.

As I said, the Victorians had it easy. This was a Grand Tour, proletarian-style.

There was a two-hour delay at Perth before we were due to join the Kings Cross to Inverness train, but that didn't matter. The Orient-Express group's Royal Scotsman was there for cleaning, and we were given permission by a crew member - who did glance nervously at my rucksack and combats but thought better of calling the guards - to explore. Vic and I had the run of the buffet car and a carriage for an hour, and it was only when I began peering in to the cabin of the engine itself - the burgundy-liveried Windsor Castle - that our time was judged to be up.

The carriage we saw was wonderful. High-backed armchairs and sumptuous fittings harked back to the days of the gentleman traveller, though I doubted servants or shotguns would be welcomed. This was Edwardian nostalgia in the era of corporate hospitality, fine dining by rail with every conceivable Scottish motif thrown in. Golf, distillery visits and a little salmon fishing were all, it seemed, part of the Royal Scotsman experience. It was excessive, indulgent and hideously beyond our means, and I wanted some of it. In a moment of rashness, I assured Vic we would return one day.

The Inverness train was running late, and so we left the Royal Scotsman and walked into town for supplies. The most vital of these was a particular variety of Avon moisturiser, which had been recommended as the definitive midgie deterrent by a friend. He had just returned - unscathed and unbitten - from two weeks among the hill lochs of Sutherland, and had assured us that the wee beasties were terrified of the stuff. "You'll smell like a right bloody pansy but they won't come near you," he had said.

The local Boots didn't stock this remarkable potion but the assistant, who had clearly been approached before by gullible Sassenachs, directed us towards a nearby camping outlet where there were trays of it on every counter. The salesman was insistent that it was not marketed or sold as a midgie cream, but was willing to take our money all the same. The mark-up was scandalous, too, but I remembered previous encounters with the Highlands' most infamous pests and would have paid double. We ran back to the station, with a bottle of the magic elixir safely in the rucksack.

The east-coast line to Inverness is one of my favourites. The mountains grow and darken once Perth is left behind; low-lying farming land gives way to the slate grey vista of the sheep crofter, and the old iron rails, which have carried fishermen in to the north for over a century, cross countless burns and rivers. I travelled this line many times as a boy, always on the night sleeper

from London with brother and I squeezed in to a single bunk, and was in my thirties before I did so in daylight. It is a journey which, for me, encapsulates all that is Scottish and special. Only the Kyle of Lochalsh line, which crosses the Highlands from East to West, rivals it. I had promised Vic that we would make both journeys during our grand tour, and that they would be ample compensation for all the fishing she would have to endure.

The construction of the east-coast line was late by the standards of railway mania, but it still met with considerable opposition. In 1892, the introduction to *The Wild Sports and Natural History of the Highlands* had the following to say:

The railways driven far into wastes of trackless bog and heather, now admit countless tourists to the most retired districts. Their taste for shooting and fishing, and the charm of a freer life than can be found in the great cities, have planted castles and shooting lodges all over Scotland. But it has pressed with great severity upon all wild life especially birds and beasts like the osprey, kite and pine marten, that are rapidly approaching extinction.

The ecological impact of the railways in remoter regions was something that I rarely considered during my journeys, though I probably should have done. The benefits of the railways, for me, always outweighed the losses. Trains democratised travel in an age when the poor got a rough deal in all other aspects of everyday life, they brought fresh food to regions that had previously gone without, they mobilised a workforce and enabled the creation of a football league. Trains opened up an island to its inhabitants, and only rarely did I consider the cost. The castles and shooting lodges which once outraged locals are now part of Scotland's romance, and any environmental consequences have long since been surpassed by the effects of motorways, North Sea oil-drilling, air travel and an endless stream of 4x4s along the A9. If Victorian railway mania carved up the British countryside, subsequent generations have managed to screw it up beyond all recognition. It's no defence, but it is the truth.

If the landscape had been ruined, it didn't appear so from our National Express carriage. Vic was entranced, and so was I. The rivers held water but didn't look especially high, and we saw anglers everywhere - in the Garry and Tummel at Pitlochry, in the Spey at Kingussie, and on streams and burns whose names we didn't know. Vic pointed out that none of them appeared to be reeling in any fish, and so I explained that this was Scotland, and that they were fishing for salmon and that sometimes these salmon weren't in the river, and when they were in the river they weren't really supposed to feed. "I see," she said. "So why exactly are we here?"

As the sky darkened we passed through Inverness, and then circuitously round the Beauly and Cromarty Firths to Alness. The route by road is much shorter here, and car drivers since 1982 have been able to cross the firth on the Kessock Bridge, a kilometre-long cable construction of German design. Before then, an ancient ferry had served visitors to the remote north-east for centuries. When the railway-builders arrived, engineers took the longer route via Beauly, and it was this that we followed.

The beauty of the Inverness and Perth railway, as shown in the
Illustrated London News *in 1863.*

Shortly before reaching Alness we crossed the Ault
Graat, a small and tumbling stream running in to the
Cromarty Firth, from which I once caught my first
salmon. The river is a quiet one, ignored by local and
visiting anglers alike, but is rich in both fish and folklore.
It was here that the legend of the Lady of Balconie
began, in the shadow of the Black Rock of Novar. A
young woman who lost her looks in childhood through
a terrible illness is said to have made a pact with *domh-
null dubh*, the devil himself, offering her eternal soul for
restored beauty. Later, a visiting Englishman became

bewitched by her, and perished in her pursuit. Local mythology has it that she can be heard by the river at night, wailing after him. An old poem offers a warning to visitors:

> *They named it Aultgraad - Ugly Burn*
> *This water through the crevice hurled*
> *Scouring the entrails of the world -*
> *Not ugly in the rising smoke*
> *That clothes it with a rainbowed cloak.*
> *But slip a foot on frost-spiked stone*
> *Above this rock-lipped Phlegethon*
> *And you shall have The Black Rock of Kiltearn*
> *For tombstone, grave,*
> *And trumpet of your resurrection.*

I've never understood the reticence of local anglers to fish the ugly burn. To me it is wild and beautiful, and the salmon run it as readily as they do the Averon or the Beauly. Perhaps the prospect of an encounter with Lucifer is a disincentive. When I fished it as a young man, though, it was the presence of bailiffs that had me looking over my shoulder.

Our host for the first three days, Cousin Ricky, met us at Alness station as the sun finally set, and immediately announced that there was a big tide at 5am and that the grilse might just be running the lower beats of the river at its height. It was mid-week, but if I wanted first run at the popular pools - the stick pool, the 'sloosh' and the road bridge - I would need to be wetting my waders an hour before the tide arrived. Ricky would be joining me, though his foot was in plaster from a mackerel-fishing calamity a week earlier, and our ghillie was to be Dougie, of whom I knew nothing. Vic went straight to bed, promising not to emerge for twelve hours.

Dougie's well-appointed but road-weary Volvo was outside by 3.45am and we were at the river ten minutes later. We worked the pool below the sluice, and then clambered over shallows to the Stick Pool, the Road Bridge and finally the estuary beat. Nothing happened, and so we did it again, and then retraced our casts a third time. Some dark fish moved up the pools at the tide's height, but we saw precious few fresh-run grilse moving up the river, and concluded that the following day's bigger tide might be 'the one'.

This was disconcertingly familiar; many years ago some friends and I fished the Welsh rivers for sewin, and became slaves to tide charts and moon phases. Each visit entailed a four-hour drive on bad roads, and almost inevitably we arrived to find the river too low or too high, the tides inopportune or the moon overly bright. We often felt that the elements were conspiring against us, and that we were spending considerable time and money throwing flies at a big empty river. Soon enough, we returned to our carp and barbel. The whiskered fishes were less fussy.

Life for the angler who chases migratory fish demands patience beyond reason, and a willingness to submit to nature's capriciousness. Dead rocks orbiting a quarter-of-a-million miles away can take on disproportionate importance. Charts and tables are scanned endlessly, skies are watched, hunches shared, but always with the knowledge that one day soon the elements will combine sympathetically and the river will fill with silver. It's a form of alchemy, or perhaps lunacy.

Biteless, we surrendered at 9am and enjoyed breakfast together. I learnt from Dougie that he was an exiled Geordie, and had visited the river each summer for twenty years before moving his family north to Ardross. I learnt too that his first salmon from the river had come in his ninth year of trying, but that he had caught more than his share since. We agreed to meet on the river that evening, and again for two more early mornings. At some point, we knew fish would move in on the tide and run the town beat. Small flies on long leaders would, my ghillie assured me, evoke a response.

And so we fished for three days at dawn and dusk. During the evenings the pools were full - not with fish, but with local anglers. That happens everywhere when there's an evening tide and the local factories and busi-nesses have finished for the day, and visiting anglers have no right to expect otherwise. The locals were friendly and accommodating, and most respected the cast-step-cast etiquette of the salmon fisher. The mornings were quieter, but there were enough anglers around at dawn to suggest that we were not alone in expecting a big run before long. We saw traditionalists with Brady bags and gye nets, local scallywags with tatty single-handed rods and bunches of maggots on their Hairy Marys, and young kids whose casting put mine to shame. One fish come to the net, a 7-pounder with sea lice on its flanks, caught by a distillery worker who fished with a roll-up permanently in his lips and a John Deere baseball cap pulled over his shaved head, but the consensus was that most of the fish were still shoaled up in the Moray Firth, waiting for rain. I hooked one on the second morning on a small orange double, a grilse of perhaps five pounds, which leapt its way around the top of the Stick Pool before throwing the hook, but that was all.

On the third morning I returned to my cousin's house to find our rucksack packed, and Vic waiting patiently. She gently reminded me that we were supposed to be travelling, and that nobody would read a book about non-existent salmon. Before we left to travel north-wards, though, Ricky took us out to the pier at Cromarty, in the shadow of the oil rigs at Nigg. It was here, a week earlier, that my cousin had tripped and bro-ken a bone in his foot whilst catching mackerel. Having failed so miserably to land a salmon, we needed to catch a few fish before returning to the East-coast line, and Ricky knew that Cromarty would provide. There were hordes of gulls and kids there - two sure signs that the fish are around, too. We caught coalies and a solitary mackerel that had evidently lost its shoal, and then took the ferry back across the firth. By early-afternoon Vic and I were on the platform at Alness waiting for the Dingwall train.

Alness once had a fully-functioning station, with a ticket collector and wrought iron roofing and all the usual appendages of the Victorian railway builders. I first pulled in there as an excited five-year-old in 1974, and could remember the moment well. My mother, who grew up in the village in the Fifties and early Sixties, had told me of the steam trains she had boarded there as a child, and of the old stationmaster, with whom she and a school pal had shared their scrumped plums one after-noon. At least some of the old station's grandeur survived in to my own childhood, though I did not know until years later that the station had already closed for over a decade in the Beeching era, and had re-opened only a year before my arrival (I suspect those two events were unconnected).

For almost a century Alness Station, like so many in that part of the world, was the central point of the village, the hub which connected its people to an outside world. In the aftermath of the second war the arrival of the motor car, and then the thundering A9 to Wick, did for many of the stations on the Far North Line. Once again, the march of modernity and the ruthlessness of Richard Beeching proved to have effects far beyond the lifting of neglected railway lines.

Dingwall station's finest days were during WWII when the region was overtaken by the military, but it did survive the cuts of the Sixties. It sits at the junction of the Far North and Kyle of Lochalsh lines, and countless Highland tourists pass through to this day. The hotel has long gone but the station has a pub attached to it - The Mallard - and though the platforms boast new LED screens, there is enough wood and iron to recall its past. We had decided to head for Wick, via Lairg, but took a bus first to Strathpeffer - a Victorian spa village hidden in the Highlands, which once had its own railway station, and later a dance hall where my mother misspent her teens and her sister Moira bagged herself a husband.

There were trout to be caught in the hills, in Lochs Ussie, Achilty and Achonachie, but few Victorian visitors to Strathpeffer had spotty wee brownies on their minds. The healing powers of its sulphur-rich mineral waters were nationally-renowned, and in the last decade of the nineteenth century the Strathpeffer Express brought visitors from as far away as London. It is not unreasonable to suspect that more than one Victorian gentleman deposited his wife at the steam room or pump house whilst chasing salmon, and this unlikely Highland village became a regular stop for those on their own grand tour.

Vic and I didn't succumb to a mud bath, but we did visit the station. This closed in 1946 when the spa trade waned but a local trust maintains it and the station building now houses a genteel café and gift shops. The building itself has changed little, but the tracks were finally lifted in 1951, and the route of the old Express is just discernible beneath a canopy of trees. Vic, whose interest in Victorian history goes far beyond travelling fishermen, wanted to stay longer. The architecture of the village - an incongruous mixture of nineteenth-century opulence, traditional pavilions and Bavarian towers - deserved more attention than I was willing to give it, but there were fish to catch. We returned to Dingwall, on a bus that was anything but express-like. The following morning a train would take us north, to Lairg and beyond.

Lairg is a remote inland settlement, and received its railway station during the 1800s in an attempt to open up the more desolate parts of Sutherland. It worked, temporarily, and hotels and lodges once catered to large numbers of visiting sports, who trolled the lochs and cast for salmon in the river. Today the village has a population of only seven hundred, and much of its trade is associated with the huge sheep auctions it hosts. It sits at the south-eastern end of Loch Shin, and a thriving angling club has a headquarters and a dozen or so white and green clinkers moored up on its banks. I had used these many times before, during a particularly savage five-year spell of ferox fever, and it was good to be back in saner circumstances. It was the first time in a decade that I had arrived at Shin without a van full of echo sounders, life jackets and similarly-afflicted psychos.

The loch itself is either nineteen or seventeen miles long, depending on who you ask, and is a long and narrow glacial scar, carved during the ice ages. In the 1950s the Scottish Hydro-Electric Company created the Lairg Dam at its southern end, and this created a second smaller body of water below, known now as Little Loch Shin. The famous Falls of Shin are found further down the valley, but we chose not to visit them - not because they aren't beautiful or astonishing - they are - but because they are now owned by Al Fayed and the Harrods Empire. We spoke to two villagers about this, and they both stared at their feet and muttered about travesties and thieving Egyptians. Twenty years earlier I would have railed against capitalist bastards and organised an unruly protest, but my balaclava and army surplus jacket disappeared about the same time as the Poll Tax and it was easier to just go fishing. Vic and I agreed to give the falls a wide berth.

Our attentions lay with the trout, and both lochs can be prolific. Big fish have been known to appear on occasion, including the cannibalistic monsters I once chased, but for most of Shin's anglers the 'breakfast broonies', three-to-a-pound, are sought with traditional loch tactics. This entails a boat, a drogue and a team of wet flies cast in to the drift. The guidebooks boast of twenty fish in a day, and in years past I had come close to emulating this, but it was not to be on this visit. Strong winds pushed down the loch and the boats were out of bounds.

White caps were forming froth on the shore, and the sky was bright and cloudless. We found a sheltered bay below the angling club's HQ, and lost an afternoon drowning worms and thrashing flies in the margins, but the trout were elusive, and the day was saved only by spinning with a small mepps - the piscatorial equivalent of punching below the belt.

As the sun dropped behind Ben More we concluded that our own breakfast would be bought rather than caught. We walked back to the village, stopping for a speculative and ultimately fruitless cast in the little loch, and found our B&B. Over supper and scotch, I promised Vic we would go back for a ferox one day, but she was less than keen, and suggested that a return to Strathpeffer might be rather more fun. I couldn't disagree.

Ricky called later that night, and he had a plan. Our vague itinerary had involved taking the Far North Line to its conclusion at Wick, and finding our way across the Kyle of Tongue and along the coast to Cape Wrath - a mere eighty miles by road, but a formidable distance for two tourists with no car and dwindling supplies of cash. There, the wild brown trout of Durness would be waiting. The absence of any railway lines between the two would not stop us, and the prospect of a long bus journey or a fortuitous attempt at hitch-hiking had been broached.

My cousin had a better idea. He and Dougie were up for some fun, and our ghillie's long-suffering Volvo would be waiting for us at Wick the following afternoon, if that appealed. It did. Vic and I caught the morning train from Lairg, and followed the east coast to Scotland's remotest station.

It was a new journey for me, and a memorable one. The railway rejoined the coast at Golspie, and travelled north through stops at Dunrobin Castle, Brora, Helmsdale and the two cottages of Altnabreac. This far north the landscape changed once more, the mountains giving way to a peat bog wilderness known as the Flow Country. Vic and I attempted to take some photographs but the blur of a moving train hampered our efforts, and eventually the batteries died.

We crossed rivers with names I'd never heard before and others like the Helmsdale that are the lexicon of the salmon fisher. Two weeks earlier I'd got drunk with Edwyn Collins and Grace Maxwell, who live on its banks. There were dizzy promises of a holiday there one day, and on first sight of its waters we knew we would have to accept their kind offer.

A couple of hours after leaving Lairg our train pulled in to the old Norse port of Thurso. There, a ferry links the Scottish mainland to Stromness, and there are also boats to Norway and Finland, but in recent years the local economy has relied upon the Dounreay Nuclear Power Plant. We thought about stopping to explore but Dougie and his Volvo would be waiting and so we pressed on to Wick.

The train backed up via Georgemas Junction and then we were there, at the last buffer of the Far North Line. Inverness felt a long way behind us, and the determination of the nineteenth-century railway builders to tame the landscape and connect the people of Caithness to a progressive world was palpable. For the first time in all the journeys I had undertaken, the scale of this great engineering feat was fully apparent. The iron lines beneath us linked this peaty, wind-swept frontier to London, to Cornwall, to every corner of the island, and it felt remarkable. Before the railways arrived, Wick might as well have been on a different planet to the emerging cities of Victoria's Britain.

We sat on a wall outside and wondered how many navvies had perished in this venture. Vic suggested that the cold would probably have got to them if nothing else had, and I did notice at this point that the wind coming in from the North Sea was particularly vicious. Minutes later, Dougie's Volvo chugged rheumatically into the car park. The ghillie and the cousin had arrived, and we were heading west.

FISHING IN NEW GALLOWAY
BY NORMAN WILKINSON R.I.

LMS **SCOTLAND** for **HOLIDAYS** **LNER**

Chapter VI

The Grand Tour - Part II

I am sure we would have enjoyed the journey from Wick towards Durness, but both of us fell asleep as soon as Dougie pulled out of the station car park. A tangle of rods and bags and nets poked at us with every bump in the road, but I remember nothing of the journey until Ricky shook me wake and announced that we were minutes away from the Cape Wrath Hotel. We were once more among the mountains, but the skyline was lower than it had been further south, and the landscape stark. The wind buffeted us as we barrelled along, and I was sure I could sense a hint of the sea in the air. Even the industrious Victorian railway builders had resisted this corner of Scotland, but the lochs we were visiting had once been among those most-prized by the touring gentlemen. The trout of Durness were and are the most remote to be found on the British mainland, but for over a century they have been visited by those willing to travel along wild single roads - be it by pony, carriage, or Volvo.

The lochs around Cape Wrath and Durness are numerous, famed for their wild and large brown trout and fabulously rich in limestone and mythology. Every tale I had ever read about these waters seemed to include a ghost story or equally implausible supernatural event, and yet our first encounter with this primitive place gave them immediate credibility. Some of the best of these were recounted in R. Macdonald Robertson's 1948 book, *Wade the River, Drift the Loch*, in which the author recounted the tales of one of Sutherland's finest old small-holders, Alexander Gunn. Gunn claimed to have been visited by the ghost of a dead Australian visitor in a remote cottage, and to have seen similar inexplicable spectra among the sheep and mists of Kinlochbervie, but his encounter with a mermaid is my favourite:

On old Christmas night 1900 I was going around after sheep between Sheigra and Sandwood Loch. While walking along the edge of the rocky headlands I noticed that one of my sheep had fallen down a gully about three miles west of Sandwood Loch, and as it was low tide I descended the cliff towards the sea shore to take it up. When I reached the bottom my collie dog let out an agonised howl as it crouched in terror close in to my feet, with hair bristling, ears set back and tail between its legs.

I looked up. What I saw was so sudden and unexpected that it took my breath away, for to my astonishment, I observed right above me what I took to be a human reclining on a ledge of rock only about six or seven feet from where I stood. Then I realised it was a mermaid! So impressed was I that I can to this day distinctly recall her appearance which left a vivid picture on my mind which I can never forget, old man that I am. She was no grey seal; she was a real mermaid - a bonnie lassie, clear in complexion as ever I saw. Her hair was reddish-yellow in colour, and curly; and she had a wreath of seaweed around her neck. She had greenish-blue eyes and arched eyebrows, and she stared at me with a kind of frightened expression on her face. She did not speak. I sensed the situation right away. She could not move until the high tide came. She was marooned on the rock on which she rested.

It is all too difficult to describe, but she was the size of an ordinary young human being, with the same features, but she had an arched back. She was very beautiful - ravishingly so! For minutes only, the mermaid and I gazed at one another; then realising that what I saw was supernormal, I took to my heels in terror.

You may all scoff at me as much as you choose, and attribute this story to drink if you will. But I saw a real mermaid off Ruadh an Fhir Leithe, and I will not depart from my story for any man on earth. If only my dog were alive today he would corroborate my story in his own canine language. What I saw was real.

As we pulled up at the general stores in Durness's main street, Vic woke up.

We were roughing it overnight at the Sango Sands camping and caravan park, in a cheap two-man tent. I had read about the 70 mph winds that can sweep across the site, which is situated above a deserted white beach on the cliffs, and knew that it could be an uncomfortable stay - and so we stocked up on pasties, chocolate and spare gas canisters for the stove. Gentlemen anglers in the past might have opted for the Cape Wrath Hotel, which was built for the Duke of Sutherland in the late 1700s, and has been both private dwelling and boarding house, but it was being refurbished when we visited and funds were dwindling. I had also read a review when planning the trip which likened it to both a monastery and the hotel in *The Shining*, and so none of us were overly disappointed. By morning, we would all change our minds.

There was no time to cast a fly, and we agreed we'd make an early start the following day. Instead we wandered aimlessly around Balnakiel Craft Village. This is situated in old Ministry of Defence buildings, and was intended as an early warning station in the event of nuclear attack. Now it offers pottery, books, all manner of hand-crafted goods and a chocolaterie. We were told that it had been reclaimed by locals in the Sixties, and there is a distinct hippy vibe about the place. Once again, I assured Vic that we would come back.

The night passed unpleasantly. The infamous winds were relentless, and our tent suffered. Sleep was impossible, and so we ate and talked and shivered. Jack Nicholson didn't burst through the entrance hissing 'here's Johnny',

but it felt like he might have done at any point, and the first tentative rays of morning light were welcome. Before sunrise, Dougie and Ricky had abandoned us for the back of the car, and it took three rounds of tea to revive them. By 8am we had decamped, and were stringing up fly rods on the banks of Loch Borallie.

Borallie is one of the larger lochs in the region, found up a path behind the hotel on raised land. A glance beyond the hotel reveals the shoreline, but I found it hard to take my eyes off the loch itself. For twenty or thirty yards all round it, the margins are shallow and clear, with a hint of limestone green. Beyond them, the loch shelves off suddenly to unknown depths and the water blackens. Ricky told me that at least one WWII bomber could be found at its bottom.

My cousin's broken foot had worsened since I'd seen him, and he decided not to fish. Instead, he would take photographs and make tea, and in all likelihood polish off the remaining food while we looked for trout. Vic had no intentions of wading amongst the wreckage of aeroplanes or the skeletal remains of unfortunate pilots, and took to the hills to read and write - in a month's time she would be starting her Creative Writing Masters Degree, and the wilds of Durness seemed as good a place as any to find inspiration. Dougie and I went fishing.

My Geordie friend, in spite of possessing knees as questionable as his car, charged into the margins and worked his way leftwards. I did likewise, but went right. On local advice we fished long light leaders with dry flies. There was no hatch evident, so we prospected with Hare's Ears and Terry's Terrors, and failed to raise a single trout all morning. The wind precluded long casting, and so I waded to the edge of the drop-off, and tried teams of nymphs along the ledge, and this fared similarly.

I wasn't wearing a watch but it felt like lunchtime, and so I found Vic, and we returned to the car for a break. Rick informed us that another angler had stopped for 'a blether' on his way to a different loch, and that we now knew that Durness had baked for the previous month and the trout were off the feed.

By late afternoon the wind had dropped and Dougie had found a small pod of feeding trout halfway up the northerly shore. I followed him, and all too briefly we enjoyed the bounty for which these lochs are famous. The fish were big - 2-pounders and above - and rose freely to the very same flies that had failed us that morning.

As quickly as it had begun, it was over. Rods were dismantled and nets dried in the heather. Over a final cup of tea, Dougie announced that we should have paid extra and used the boats, and fished big lures in the deep water. He knew a man who had once done that, and who had taken thirty of these magnificent trout home with him at the end of his day. Vic and I agreed that one day soon we would come back, and risk the wrath of mermaids and Jack Nicholson and the ghosts of the airmen, and catch the fish that had eluded us.

We wanted to travel West, but doing so by train necessitated a detour back to Dingwall, and Dougie and Rick were happy to take us there en route to Alness. In the late-1800s and early 1900s, designs had been drawn up for an ambitious network of rail lines taking in Ullapool and the furthest corners of Sutherland, but these plans were never realised, and the west coast is poorly served by rail to this day. At Dingwall, Vic and I could at least follow the Kyle Line to its dramatic conclusion at Lochalsh, and I could make good on my promise that we would take this spectacular journey. The following morning, that is precisely what we did.

The sixty-three miles of the Kyle Line were laid between 1862 and 1897, and join the east coast to the west at the narrowest point in the Highlands. Like the Looe Line that had taken me to the nauseous world of English shark fishing, the Kyle Line was one of very few that was awarded a reprieve after being threatened with mothballing by Beeching - most agree that it was saved because of the promise of North Sea oil. Today, only the Dingwall and Kyle stations are staffed, but the route is still a popular one and would once have been used by countless tourists and anglers making their way from Inverness to the lochs of the West Coast and further on to Skye.

Twelve miles beyond Dingwall we passed Garve, a tiny station alongside a huge loch where I once caught a tiny pike on a dry Greenwell's Glory. From there the line passes through Lochluichart and Achnasheen before reaching the route's summit at Luib, 646 feet above sea level. The descent towards the west coast is a gentle one and is wonderfully scenic, and the first sight of Loch Carron is especially memorable. This had once been the intended conclusion to the line, but the early pioneers pressed on through difficult terrain towards Kyle.

We arrived in time for lunch but first explored the station itself, a listed building that has been sympathetically-restored. The tide was in, so my spinning rod was strung up and we tried for mackerel in the harbour. Nothing stirred.

At this point the paucity of the west-coast rail network finally scuppered us. I wanted to go north, to Ullapool and its harbour, its gigantic ferox trout and the finest fish and chip shop in the Highlands, but without a car there was no way to get there. Further south we could have jumped on to the Mallaig Line towards Rannoch and Oban and Mull, but that too was beyond our reach. There was little choice but to get back on the Kyle Line, and find our way to Loch Ness.

I knew that Ness offered an opportunity to chase some monsters - not the humped-backed prehistoric variety, but the kind that might just be dredged up with a deep running spinner trolled behind a boat. In the late-1990s, in Graham's Tackle Shop in Inverness, I had pocketed the business card of a trout guide who offered boat trips on Scotland's most famous water. I still had it, and as our train climbed towards Luig I phoned him and found that he was still around, and still catching trout. He had two spots free for the following day, and so we took them.

Our guide was Alex - a wiry, weathered old boy in checked shirt and baseball hat - and we met him in the lobby of the Loch Ness Clansman Hotel the following morning. The guiding operation was run through the hotel, which has its own jetty on the northern shoreline at Brackla, but the boat was his own. My first impressions were mixed - the craft itself was a decommissioned Norwegian lifeboat called *The Time Bandit*, which had begun its life on inland fjords in the 1940s, and seemed more than robust enough for a day chasing trout on Ness. Its fittings, however, were less satisfactory - plastic garden chairs, a broken echo-sounder and a curious mixture of boat rods, fly rods and rusty spinners covered the decks. Vic was apprehensive, but we had paid our money and had nowhere else to go.

Four of us would be fishing: Vic and I were joined by a father and son who were, I think, Swiss holidaymakers. Neither of them spoke during the next four hours, and we exchanged only benign smiles and a parting handshake at the end of the day. It was weird.

Alex took us along the northern shore, towards Urquhart Castle. Four rods were used: two deep running lures were dropped from the back, and our ghillie suggested these might pick up any large trout or salmon lurking in the black water; on the sides he set up a light multiplier outfit with a silver Toby, and a team of wet flies fished deep on a double-handed salmon rod with sinking line. The tackle itself had a boot-fair feel to it, but Alex clearly knew his loch and I quickly overcame my tackle snobbery; the tattiness of the equipment was the least of our worries, and wouldn't stop the trout from biting. The bright sky and hot weather would see to that.

We were too late in the season to reasonably expect a ferox or salmon to appear. Five years of hard-bitten specimen trout fishing had taught me the importance of cloud, low temperatures and endless quantities of time. We had none of these, and so our day on Loch Ness became a relaxed affair, with an outside chance of a few wee broonies for company. The first hour passed quietly.

As the boat neared Urquhart Castle, Alex announced that it was my turn to take the wheel, and suggested that it was time to summon up the fish with a wee bit of Highland magic. With that, he pulled a battered fiddle from the cabin, and launched in to a medley of reels, jigs and strathspeys, grinning widely and proclaiming that

Urquhart Castle, Loch Ness.

only traditional Scottish music could conjure up a Ness trout. Vic and I were impressed, our Swiss friends bemused, but sure enough the trout appeared.

In the next half hour the Toby and lure rods registered five bites. Two of these came to nothing, but three brownies up to a pound were enough to please the punters and prove the potency of *My Love She's But a Lassie Yet*. Deep down, I knew that the sudden arrival of the trout had more to do with the topography of the loch than Alex's musical interlude, and that this was a party trick he doubtless used every day of the week, but I was happy to be hoodwinked. The ghillie had provided fish and a little Celtic magic, and it didn't matter that we had all been well and truly fiddled.

I returned to the rods and Alex took the wheel as we turned back up the northern shore towards the hotel.

High in the hills above the castle, on a lay-by on the A82, a young man played the bagpipes as we chugged past. This, we were told, was Spud the Piper, and he played there all the time. The trout vanished, and our ghillie entertained us instead with tales of the ferox that had come to his boat in the past, his love of hill running and highland games, and his family's involvement in traditional folk music. There were jokes too, including an especially poor one about Nessie meeting an atheist, the details of which escape me now. All too soon, we were on dry land.

Our fishing was over, but we had a free afternoon before it was time to catch a train to Perth and so took a bus to the western end of the Great Rift, below the end of Loch Ness. There, the remains of the short-lived Invergarry-Fort Augustus Railway can be found. This line ran from 1903 to the 1930s between Spean Bridge and Augustus, passing Lochs Lochy and Oich, and taking Edward VII and rich landowners west for 'the season'. Long before the ruthless economics of Richard Beeching, most locals declared that the line should never have been built, and many regard it as a vanity project for the old king. In many ways, it typified the heady years of Scottish railway mania, when tracks were laid for no better reason than taking the wealthy to their salmon, stags and lodges. Today, the Invergarry Station Project is attempting to restore the old station and clear a path along the route. When we visited, only the raised land where the tracks once were hinted at an indulgent past, snaking away past Loch Oich and towards the west coast.

We had afternoon tea in a café on the banks of the Caledonian Canal, and watched as a succession of steamers

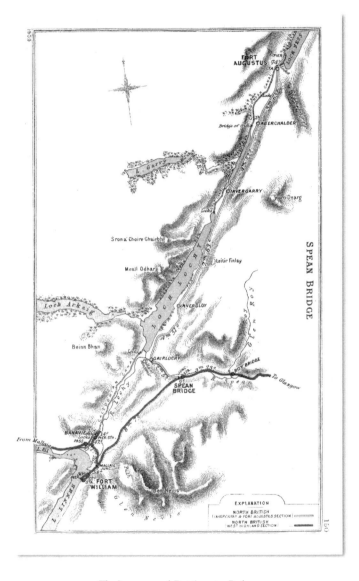

The Invergarry and Fort Augustus Railway.

and yachts negotiated the locks as they sailed towards Ness. From where we sat, two of the three incarnations of Scottish travel could be seen - the boats that have carried pleasure-seekers from one end of the Great Glen to the other for centuries and the A82 trunk road which was built with depression-era labour in the thirties. Only the railway has disappeared from view, and with it has gone an age when a gentleman could load his first-class carriage with Pall Mall rod cases and servants, a shotgun or two, perhaps his wife and family, and embark on his grand tour of the north.

I shouldered the rucksack and rods, and Vic gathered up our bags. We turned our backs to Rannoch Moor and the lochs of the west, and fishing adventures that would have to wait for another day. It was time to go home.

Chapter VII

South Parade Pier

When my parents were courting, my virtuous Highland mother once asked my father whether she was 'his first'. Dad's reply, according to family legend, went along the lines of 'maybe - were you on Southsea Common in 1958?'

True or apocryphal, it is one of my father's favourite after-dinner tales, and I have heard him tell it many times - always late in the evening and occasionally peppered with imaginative flourishes if the Glenmorangie has lost its cork.

My mother was not on the Common that night - she didn't leave Scotland until the late-1960s, when she boarded the East Coast sleeper to Euston with a husband and twin boys for company - but the grassy expanses of Southsea and its two Victorian piers do belong in my genetic past. It was among the slot machines and bars, in the age of Bill Haley and Duck's Arse Hairstyles, that my Dad caroused as a teenager, perfecting the hedonism that would later earn him his Navy non-de-plume, 'the coiled spring'.

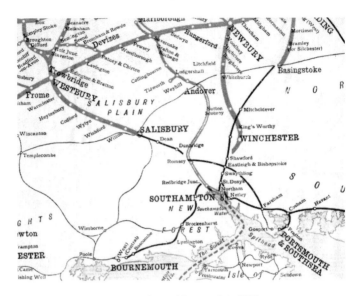

Lines in and around Portsmouth in 1925.

It was in South Parade Pier's ballroom that my brother and I took tentative steps towards rock-and-roll anonymity, as teenage participants in the local Battle of the Bands. And, it was on the same pier's end on an icy Saturday morning that Chris and I fished with our granddad, catching pollock in what were our final hours with him, though we didn't know it then.

So, Southsea's common and piers have been etched, hazily but indelibly, on my recollection of childhood for a very long time. I didn't return for over twenty years - not deliberately but simply because I had no reason to - yet the lure of sun-baked ragworm and kiss-me-quick hats eventually drew me back. Like thousands of Victorian pleasure-seekers before me, I took the train to the south coast for an August bank holiday. Unlike my predecessors, I was concerned only with catching fish and - just perhaps - resurrecting the spirit of the infamous Coiled Spring.

The new railways took the masses to the beaches and piers of Britain from the 1840s onwards. In that decade, resorts were established in Weston-super-Mare, Blackpool, Eastbourne, Torquay and fourteen other unsuspecting seaside settlements, all ill-prepared for an influx of factory-dwelling townsfolk with cholera and knotted handkerchiefs. By the end of Victoria's century dozens of other locations had embraced the new social mobility, and bank holidays saw thousands decamping to the coast for a day of deck-chairs, buckets and spades, variety shows and even a little fishing. Southsea's pier opened to great fanfare in 1879, and travellers arriving on the London to Portsmouth line could board steamers to the Isle of Wight from the pavilion at the pier's end. High diving competitions, daily concert parties and fireworks amused the holidaymakers, but the 600-foot wooden pier also offered anglers the chance to cast in to deep waters.

Southsea had a reputation as early as the 1880s for flatfish, garfish and the loathsome sea scorpions, but it was the construction in the inter-war years of an offshore anti-submarine boom - a steel and concrete structure in which crabs and prawns found shelter - that pulled in the bass which made that part of the Solent famous. Bass became the target species of shore and boat anglers in the Fifties and Sixties, and the Southsea Sea Angling Club built a boat compound and headquarters (with lounge bar, billiards room and tackle storage) within a hundred yards of the pier itself. Holidaymakers could

take up temporary membership for five shillings a week, though most would have chosen to hurl feathers and worms off the pier end for anything that swam. Those who availed themselves of the Angling Club's boats would have been serious sorts with an agenda that began and ended with bass. On the pier, however, there was beer and candyfloss and the stars of the Gaiety Ballroom to contend with. Serious bass men in the Fifties would probably not have succumbed to Arthur English's 'Ring Out the Bells' or Reg Dixon's 'Jump for Joy' - but thousands did, and fished for a few hours whilst there.

During the train journey - which took me to Reading and Guilford before arriving beneath the wrought iron arches of Portsmouth and Southsea's station - I decided to follow in the footsteps of the kiss-me-quick beer-swilling pleasure-seekers, rather than the serious bass men. For the son of the Coiled Spring, it was a matter of duty.

The railways arrived in Portsmouth as early as 1847, terminating at Portsmouth Town station - a split-level four-platform terminus which remains almost in its entirety today and is now known as Portsmouth and Southsea. The rail company recognised the desirability of extending the line to the coast, but were prevented from doing so by military authorities who would not allow fortifications between Old Portsmouth and Portsea to be breached. This changed when South Parade Pier opened in the 1870s, and began operating a ferry service to the Isle of Wight. Non-stop travel to the coast was more desirable than ever, and so the Southsea Railway Company was formed by Mayor Edwin Galt, and a line constructed between Fratton and Southsea. A station was built close to the pier at Granada Road, and the smallest railway company in the country (with the shortest track, at 1¼ miles in length) opened for business in 1885.

Galt's project depended upon the co-operation of the two firms running the Portsmouth to London line - the London, Brighton and South Coast Railway, and London and South West Railway. Within a year, both had bought the Mayor out, and the Southsea line immediately came under intense financial scrutiny; while the trams from the city centre remained unreliable it thrived, but by the beginning of the twentieth century visitors to Southsea shunned it for newer modes of transport. As men marched to war in the summer of 1914, the line became irretrievably unprofitable and in 1923 the tracks were finally lifted. There is little now to suggest that it ever existed; a portion of platform can be found on private property and the route can be recognised in the gaps between buildings in Goldsmith Avenue and Albert Road, but the three bridges which carried passengers to the coast were demolished when the tracks were removed, and Galt's railway is all but gone.

For this reason, my journey ended at Portsmouth and Southsea. The station is now owned by South West Trains, and is also used by Southern Trains and First Great Western. Such shared use is now a matter of economic necessity, and appears to cause few problems, but this wasn't always so; in the 1850s disputes between rival rail companies led to fighting, temporary strikes and closures on the Portsmouth line, and a horse-bus was provided when the trains did not run.

This would have been preferable to the claustrophobic swelter of the carriage which took me on the last leg of the journey. It was oppressively warm, standing room

only, but the coup-de-grace was having a short stocky gentleman (clearly a Portsmouth FC supporter, I surmised from the tattoos on his scalp) lodged under one armpit as I clung to the overhead handrail. I chose not to declare my allegiance to Southampton FC, or my hero-worship of Matthew Le Tissier - men who submit their craniums to ink-filled needles rarely, in my experience, engage in football small talk with the enemy.

My guest house was typical of many found in the maze of streets constructed in the early years of Victoria's reign by Thomas Ellis Owen. A smiling but silent landlord led me up four flights of stairs to the smallest room I have ever paid money to stay in. A single bed took up two-thirds of its allotted space, and my rucksack filled what was left. There was a television and a sink with a boiler above it, and a bedside table piled high with out-of-date TV guides. My host finally spoke, perhaps by way of distraction, as I contemplated the facilities. "You're the writer, ain't you? The one who phoned up saying he was doing a book. Well, I don't know what you're used to but this ain't the bleedin' Ritz."

He laughed at this. I smiled, thinly. "Anyway, breakfast is at seven. We offers a comprehensive menu. Full English or fuck all." He left then, but I could still hear him chuckling to himself when he'd reached the floor below. I decided that it was time to walk over the common and return to the pier.

The streets of Southsea were buzzing, and it seemed all life was there. Holidaymakers wandered the pavements, listless afternoon drinkers sat outside wine bars and elderly residents leaned from upstairs windows. It was these streets that were most damaged by Hitler's bombs, and the architecture is a curious mixture of patched-up early Victoriana and post-war pre-fab. There was beauty and chaos and a whiff of degeneracy, and I knew that the Coiled Spring would have loved it.

If the streets were lively, the common was positively seething. I had unwittingly arrived during Southsea's annual kite festival, and beneath the display were hundreds of enthusiasts, accompanied by the ubiquitous burger and drink vans. Closer to the shore, between the sea and the model village, a second crowd had gathered. Here, a young band played covers of old Jam numbers in aid of a local charity. Young Mods danced at the front, defiantly wearing their fish-tail parkas in the heat. I stopped for a smoke, and enjoyed a note-perfect rendition of *Town Called Malice*. If I had come to recapture some of my youth, as well as that of my father, it seemed that my past was in on the arrangement, and was coming in search of me too.

Every visit I made to South Parade Pier as a boy began

with the purchase of a quarter-pound of ragworm from the shop at the end of the pier. The service at this shaker-styled wooden hut was always unreliable, they were frequently out of bait, and when there were sufficient supplies it was usually straggly, sun-baked and dying. My first surprise was that the tackle hut had moved to the entrance of the pier on the main road - but it was reassuring to find that the service was as quirky as ever. Business had not been brisk during the wet summer, and there was no worm, and precious little tackle. "I ain't got much in," the owner told me. "Too much rain this summer, season's been fucked mush."

He was right - the shelves were almost empty. I left with a frozen mackerel and some feathers, and was told that the garfish were in and would feed on strips of fish. "When you get your first one, though, chop it up for bait. That mackerel's getting on a bit."

There is nowhere on earth quite like the end of the pier on a summer afternoon. The wooden platform from which the old ferry used to disembark was crawling with anglers of every persuasion. Hard-core bass men had claimed the prime spots, casting live baits far out to sea beyond the breakers. Holidaymakers dropped hand lines and fiddled ineptly with telescopic outfits of Far-Eastern origin. Between them all, the pier rats - semi-feral kids with school holiday tans and a chattering simian vocabulary - chased the shoals of small fish that moved between the pier's uprights. I found a gap on the east side of the lower platform, albeit a small one, next to a man who was filling a bucket with garfish. Quickly, I was among them too.

The method was simple, as good methods always are,

and slithers of fish beneath a pike float were quickly seized. Within an hour I had landed six and missed as many, and my neighbour and I were establishing a reputation among the pier rats as the Garfish Kings. Our techniques were quickly emulated, and my tackle box raided for floats. As the sun dipped and the day began to cool, my neighbour announced that he had to leave - he had, I learned, just joined the Navy and was expected back at base - and so I surrendered my spot too, and decided to talk to the bass men. The pier rats soon filled the vacuum, and the garfish kept coming.

The bass men were Polish and Croatian, and worked in sea front hotels - though they weren't keen to tell me which ones. These same hotels, it transpired, paid them in cash for any bass they caught, and so this was a small-scale and tax-free cottage industry. When they were required back in the kitchens and lobbies, friends would replace them and keep the industry ticking over. While talking to them, and sharing their beer, a 3-pounder attached itself to one of their lines, and was promptly dispatched with a knife through its skull. I made my excuses and left, vowing not to eat bass during my stay - black market or otherwise.

Their beer had made me hungry and so I walked back in to the heart of the town to find a restaurant. *Truffles* seemed to provide all that the son of the Coiled Spring could want; seafood, alcohol in abundance and a room full of people bent on irresponsible fun. I joined them, devoured paella, and began an evening of degeneracy. This was a local's bar - everyone knew each other, and so they vetted me for suitability to join them at the bar. The concept of the book baffled all, but any writing credentials were judged better than none and I was invited - six beers in to the evening - to contribute something meaningful to the quotations blackboards hung in the toilets. I don't remember what I put - but I suspect it was something about coiled springs and eastern Europeans and the potency of Hampshire paella.

By the early hours the blinds were drawn and the lights turned low, but we locals stayed on (I had been accepted when the empty bottles in front of me had reached double figures). Conversations are hard to recall but took a distinctly theatrical turn; there was a toast to Peter Sellars who had been born only yards away, a monologue from an out-of-work actor who was growing a Charles Manson-esque beard for his next role, and scurrilous Hollywood gossip from a gentleman who owned a business renting military costumes to film companies. I vowed to return every weekend and declared it the finest bar in the northern hemisphere - an honour I have bestowed more than once before - and when it was time to leave a charming lady with excessive piercings pointed me towards the guest house and offered to see me home. I declined, knowing that the Coiled Spring might have acted differently.

In the morning, and after a memorable breakfast, I returned to the pier for an hour before my train arrived. The bass were still being pursued, this time by a different shift of Poles and Croats, and the pier rats had returned to chase the shoals around the uprights. Several fished with pike floats and strips of fish, and it was clear that the Garfish Kings of yesterday had been deposed. It was early, but the beach was filling up with deck-chairs and beach towels, and the piped music of the Gaiety Bar sang out as temperatures rose. I decided I would return to the Pier one day – perhaps in another twenty years – and knew that when I did, little would have changed.

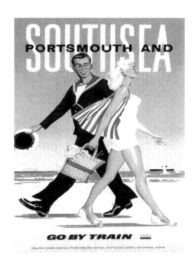

Chapter VIII

The Maggot Train

My friend Mick has always wanted to catch a twenty-pound carp on his Allcocks Wallis Wizard. Given the choice, he wants to tempt it with bread-flake or worm, using a float. Mick has caught carp bigger than twenty pounds, and smaller of course, but in recent years his fishing life has revolved around wild brown trout and an old Sharpes Eighty-Five and so the Wizard carp dream remains precisely that.

It was nearly twenty years ago that Mick shared his curious ambition with me. We were sitting on the banks of a triangular carp pool in Hampshire, watching uncatchable monsters cruise between beds of potamogeton. We agreed that it was a contrived target, but one that would be fun to realise, and we agreed also that the carp we were watching at the time were much too large for fifty-year-old bamboo.

I can remember thinking at the time that Mick's ambition was a little specific - he had drawn long on his pipe that evening and declared, "Twenty pounds exactly,

that'll do me" - but I liked it nonetheless. It was infi-
nitely preferable to the challenge I had heard about from
the banks of America's great freestone trout rivers, that of
catching twenty 20-inch trout in a day. Mick's ambition
derived from a love of old bamboo and a loyalty to Hugh
Tempest Sheringham, not blood-lust and one-upman-
ship. I knew Mick well, and if he never caught his Wizard
carp, it wouldn't bother him one jot. He's that sort of
fisherman.

I have never been one for targets myself. The simple
act of catching fish is usually enough, and I'm inept
enough an angler to be amazed whenever it happens.
I've had dalliances with dream fish - there were four
winters lost to the idea of a thirty-pound river pike, for
example - but the realisation of those dreams has never
been as important to me as just going fishing and hoping.

And, just occasionally, a very big fish has come along.

Three years ago, I was interviewed for a website. They
asked me what my perfect fishing day might be like, and
whether I had any angling ambitions left to fulfil. I gave
a flippant answer - something about catching a record
ferox trout, with Kiera Knightley as my ghillie, while
England won the Ashes on the transistor radio. They
didn't publish that answer, and I was too embarrassed to
tell them the truth.

The truth is that I have long held one single ambition
in fishing, and here it is.

I would like to catch a 14lb 6oz barbel from the
Royalty Fishery on the Hampshire Avon. It would have
to be exactly that - a fish to match the twin barbel
records from the 1930s - and not an ounce above or
below that weight. The capture would place my name

alongside those of the Aylmer Tryon and F.W.K. Wallis in the Royalty pantheon, and I could return to gudgeon and bleak and anonymity. Ideally, the barbel would bite somewhere in the Railway Pool. Oh, and my fish would have to be caught on a Wallis Wizard too.

You can see why I don't talk about it very often. It's just a dream, rather than a target. Targets are within the grasp of the determined and the resolute. Dreams, on the other hand, involve ancient barbel or net-wielding film stars, and don't happen to secondary school teachers from Swindon. And yet, thoughts of those Thirties monsters are never far from my mind when I go to Christchurch.

My efforts to bring this folly to fruition have been occasional. The Royalty is an hour-and-a-half from my house by car, and reaching the front of the queue at Davis Tackle by 7.30am has always been a challenge. When I have made the early morning dash down to Wessex, it has been with a nagging awareness that I have driven over three perfectly good, deserted barbel rivers to get there. More often I have rolled in to the House Pool's gravel car park at lunchtime, when every pitch with the remotest hint of barbel has long been taken. In recent seasons I have fished there infrequently, invariably for the pike, and so the odds on emulating Wallis and Tryon have lengthened. The pantheon has remained undisturbed.

As I travelled back from Southsea, a little fragile after my evening at Truffles, I thought of the Royalty. The chaos and noise of the pier had been amusing, but less salty waters were calling and I knew I had to visit the Hampshire Avon. I also knew that, historically-speaking, the railways were the only way to get there.

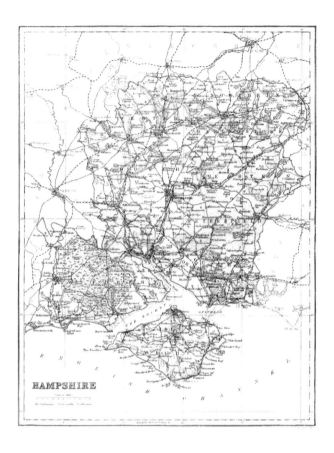

The Wessex rivers owe much to the railways, and may never have flourished without them. Until the final years of Victoria they were ostensibly salmon rivers, but that changed in the 1890s when two fishermen - the Gomm Brothers - used the new railway network to transport Thames barbel to the Dorset Stour and Hampshire Avon. On later journeys the wooden barrels in the freight carriages contained carp and tench and silver fish, all captured from the waters around Staines by rod and line.

The extent of their activities is shrouded in some mystery, but there can be little doubt that these two Londoners, working in league with a local hotelier called Newlyn, did much to transform two of the south's premier salmon rivers in to equally desirable coarse fisheries.

Their actions were timely; the Thames was about to enter an extended decline, and Midlands anglers were already deserting the polluted Trent. England's fishermen decamped to the Throop and Royalty fisheries in numbers, and the London and South-Western Railway took them there. Within forty years, the Royalty was home to record-breaking barbel catches, and the early morning train from London now brought biscuit tins full of maggots from Midlands bait farms to meet demand in the tackle shops of Ringwood and Christchurch.

And so the South-West line from London brought the fishermen, the bait, and even the fish themselves. For all these reasons, only a day after washing Southsea's sand from my shoes, I took the early morning Maggot Train from London to Christchurch, the harbour town where the two great rivers of Wessex meet.

The Wallis Wizard didn't come with me. I had secured the reserved water of the Top Weir for two days - apparently someone had cancelled - and knew that a stronger rod would be needed in the white water below the lasher. My Wizard is a newer model, early Sixties I'm told by those who study labels and tapers and the idiosyncrasies of sheet cork, but its best days are behind it and if used for ledgering it has a tendency to take on a fixed curve by mid-afternoon. Without it, the record barbel dream was redundant, albeit on a minor point of order, which took a little pressure off me and, perhaps, the occupants of the pantheon. Sometimes it is easier to enjoy fishing when failure is determined in advance.

I did pack a split-cane Avon rod, a favourite centre-pin and some floats. Nigel at the tackle shop had told me when I'd booked that the silver fish were shoaling up below the weir and there was a reasonable chance of sport from them, and perhaps the big perch which had followed them there. I also took another old railway guide to read on the train, and so the final slow miles through Sway and Brockenhurst and Hinton Admiral were given over to *Fishing in the South* by J.W.G. Tomkin. The author researched his book in 1934, and the Southern Railway Company published it in the following year. Curiously, no mention is made of Tryon's record barbel, but his notes on Christchurch are otherwise detailed.

Quite recently it has been found that the lower reaches of the Avon hold immense barbel, which actually average from 6 to 7lb, in the Royalty Fishery stretch at Christchurch. The nearest station is Christchurch, which is five minutes walk from the water and about ten minutes from the centre of the town.

Accommodation is plentiful and varied, but it may be noted that the King's Arms Hotel caters especially for anglers. The telephone number is Christchurch 69 and visiting anglers may be well advised to book in advance if they intend to stay there. The special tariff for anglers is 15/- per day all-in, including an excellent luncheon basket for those who intend to take their mid-day meals by the river.

Full particulars, conditions and tickets to fish may be obtained from the Head Water Bailiff, Mr M. Hayter . . . punts may be hired from Mr Hayter, and he also has an excellent tackle shop and can supply the forgetful or unfortunate angler with every-

thing he is likely to need on the water. The usual method of fishing is to swim the stream, and from a punt the float is allowed to trent downstream for a considerable distance.

The author's use of 'trent' as a verb in place of 'trot' is telling, and perhaps owes its origins to the Midlands anglers who began to fish the Royalty regularly between the wars, and who brought the method with them. Indeed, the first angler to catch a Royalty barbel was a Trentman named Birks who visited in 1911 with F.W.K. Wallis and Jack Bailey. These Newark and Nottingham anglers returned year after year, and their barbel catches in the Thirties are the stuff of legend. As my train lurched slowly through the final miles of the New Forest and pulled in to the modest victorian station at Christchurch, I decided I would trent my float, rather than trot it, in the following days. Wallis and his friends were the founders of the pantheon, after all, and a little sucking up couldn't hurt.

Tomkin's words suggest that little has changed since

the days of Wallis and Tryon. The Royalty's reputation as a venue for holiday anglers is a strong as ever, and the infamous crowds of the Thirties are there, three or more generations on. The tackle shop is still there, though it has moved from the bailiff's hut to its current premises on the high street, and so too is the pub - albeit re-named the Royalty Arms, and with a hand-painted sign which shows Royalty hero Jack Harrigan with a thir-teen-pound barbel in his hands. Suburbia and industry has gradually enveloped the land around the fishery, but many of the landmarks which Tomkin would have enjoyed are there still - the bends of the House Pool, the reinforced banks of the Piles, the secluded Parlour and the great iron bridge over the Railway Pool, on which a commuter train once stopped and allowed its passengers to watch one of Wallis's companions land a monster.

It is all too tempting to get swept up in the history of the place when fishing the Royalty - I certainly do - but the challenges facing the angler are very real, and wholly modern. There are the poachers in the harbour at Mudeford who net the salmon and sea trout before they enter the river, and who are hunted themselves by police using night scopes and walkie-talkies. Then there are the perennial threats to water quality of low summer flows and pollution from local industry. Talk of mink and otters is common, though the current management do much to moderate predation. Finally, there is the challenge of the fish themselves - these are canny creatures, well-versed in bolt-rigs, back-leads and other traps laid by twenty-first century specimen hunters. The Royalty barbel are as educated as any chalkstream trout, and rarely succumb to clumsy serendipity.

Right: All that remains of Edward VII's vanity line, the Invergarry to Fort Augustus Railway.

Below right: Alex, the fiddling boatman of Loch Ness.

Below: Trolling past Urquhart Castle on Loch Ness

Above: A lovely evening on South
Parade Pier.

Left: It's garfish for supper . . .

Right: Barbel fishing on the
Hampshire Avon.

Danger
No Swimming

Motor boats
operating

Sudden drop

EMILY

Above: Bells on the end of char rods.

Far left: The author boarding Emily *for a day's char fishing on Windermere.*

Left: The big pike of Low Wood!

Below: Char boat in action.

Photographs courtesy of Andrew Herd.

Above: A 21lb pike from the Dead End, Oulton.

Right: The bustling transport hub that could only be Lowestoft station.

Below: Evening light, Oulton Broad.

Sea fishing near Whitby. Above, the author tries his luck for codling at Saltwick . . .
and later has a go at 'flatty bashing' at Sandsend.

The end of the line . . .

Left: The beautiful cast-iron posts at Ellesmere station. The station is still there but the last train left nearly fifty years ago.

Below: Fishing in the ponds at Trench Farm. The ponds are in an old cutting on the Ellesmere to Wrexham line.

Bottom: The old railway bridge at Trench.

Photographs courtesy of Andrew Herd.

Wandering around with a knackered Wizard and a ball of cheese paste can, therefore, place the romantic at a distinct disadvantage. At such times, local knowledge is everything.

Angling guides have worked the banks of the Royalty for decades, but the best advice is invariably obtained in the tackle shop at the start of the day. When I first visited the Royalty, the shop's owner was 'Grumpy' Graham Pepler, a self-styled misanthrope with the lugubrious demeanour of a Rolling Stones' bass player. Irascibility is forgivable in a man who has spent decades waking before dawn to dispense tickets to bleary-eyed anglers, and in truth Grumpy was delightful and informative in equal measure, and would always know where the fish were. He has retired now, but his successor - the far from lugubrious Nigel Gray - is equally reliable. Advice from either of these gentlemen can be treated as utterances from the pantheon itself.

The barbel, it seemed, were not to be found in the Top Weir. Nigel assured me there would be a resident fish or two in the white water, but that time might be more profitably spent trotting maggots down the far bank from the pitch known as Jack's Corner. According to the local sage, the rest of the barbel were further down the fishery between Trammels and Harrigan's. The first afternoon's fishing confirmed this - the roach and dace came readily to maggots, while the cries of successful barbel hunters could be heard in the distance. I was particularly pleased to catch some roach; the Avon was once famed for them, but like many rivers has witnessed a decline. Mine were bright, scarlet-finned fish, and the biggest topped a pound.

In the evening I set up my ledger rod, and waded out in to the froth. Nigel had suggested I bounce a cube of luncheon-meat around in the white water, allowing the undertow to whip it back up under the sill, just in case a barbel was foraging. One certainly was, though it was six pounds under the size required for immortality. All the same, an eight-pound barbel is a fine fish, and she put up a thumping fight that would have reduced my old Wizard to splinters. The last of the light went as I nursed her in the margins, and after a few moments she darted in to the black.

I spent the night at the Royalty View Guest House, which has long been the preferred accommodation of visiting anglers. Residents are rarely there when the fishery or the Royalty Arms are open, and so facilities are understandably frugal. The owner - Mel Evans - is a local barbel angler who understands the idiosyncratic needs of his clientele, and so for a modest sum the angler gets a warm bed and an early breakfast, just a little local knowledge and an absence of frills.

Mel had little to offer by way of advice on my second morning. A hot still day was forecast and the barbel would be elusive, but the weir would still be full of silver if I knew where to look. I did learn that the previous owner of his guest house had been old Joe Harrop, a Royalty regular and contemporary of some of the local greats. As I left I spotted a photograph on the wall of Joe with his 13-pounder, a monster which came after a lifetime of trying. I silently hoped it had earnt him a little elbow room with Wallis and Birks, and walked back to the river.

The top weir's flow was less than the previous day, and

if the barbel were foraging there, I failed to find them. I did have one thumping bite on a ledgered halibut pellet, but the culprit weeded me before we were able to become acquainted. I suspected it was a barbel, but it could just as easily have been a chub or a carp or a salmon. A dozen repeat casts failed to elicit a similar take, and so I returned to Jack's Corner and to the roach and dace. At some point in the afternoon the float dipped more conclusively and a chub of four pounds appeared, but this was a solitary chavender among an afternoon of tiddlers.

As the sun dropped, a pair of mirror carp basked on the shallow plateau in the middle of the pool. Neither dipped their heads to feed on the corn I threw at them, and they soon cruised downstream in the warm upper layers, with an arrogance that only big carp can muster. Few things in nature are as aloof as a carp that doesn't want to know you. These two were broad, blue-backed and magnificent, and probably weighed twenty pounds. Either would have satisfied Mick's Wizardly ambitions.

Night fell and I packed away in the salmon hut. As I did so, a friend of the bailiff arrived to fish the night for perch. He carried two powerful carbon rods, each loaded with livebait tackle, in-line stone weights and lead core shock leaders. If he spotted my old bamboo, he chose not to comment.

The train journey home the following morning was slow, but that didn't matter. A new term was about to begin, and the final hours of the holiday could pass as slowly as they wished. I thought about Wallis and Tryon and Birks, and about the ruthlessness of modern perch fishing. I thought about Mick and the carp he hoped to catch, and about enormous old barbel. I thought about the Maggot Train and wondered what had happened to the biscuit tins – were they ever returned to the Midlands bait farms? Was there a stockpile of them hidden away somewhere in Bournemouth, rusting away and reeking of another generation's sawdust and ammonia?

The flat scrub of the New Forest gave way to the over-development of Southampton, and then the tracks swung north to Eastleigh. There, the train sat still for almost an hour as undisclosed problems up the line were resolved. I watched the planes landing and taking off at the adjacent airport, and remembered the ill-fated local campaign to rename it Matt Le Tissier International. Now there would have been an accolade of pantheon proportions – and the Dell faithful did call him Le God, after all.

The diesel engine finally grumbled back in to life and pulled us forward, towards the Itchen valley and beyond. Ahead lay more delays, more platform coffees, changes at Basingstoke and Reading – and then twelve weeks of teaching. Dreams of record barbel and immortality would have to wait.

Chapter IX

Windermere

It was the railways which opened up the Lake District to mass tourism. Before their arrival, roads were few and dangerous, and the packhorse track which followed the northern shore of Windermere before entering Central Lakeland would have carried few fishermen. Galloway-pony teams pioneered trade through the mountains but these were men who would have preferred the back-room betting of the inns to the niceties of a well-cast fly. Before the iron lines arrived, the few visitors were the well-heeled on their obligatory 'tour of the north'; guidebooks from the 1700s invariably described Scotland and the Lakes as one. Nevertheless, fishing was there, and was organised, for those who chose to explore. In 1792, Adam Walker described the 'convenient high road from Kendal to Ambleside, where boats, lines and baits are available for fishing, and where the game fish are perch (called bass here)', but visitors were a rarity. It took the civilising influence of the railways to offer the pleasures of the Lakeland to England's ordinary fishermen, but if the views of William Wordsworth had prevailed, it might never have happened.

Wherever I travelled during these journeys, I heard similar stories of early resistance, though they were rarely orchestrated by poets. The nineteenth-century has a reputation among historians for being progressive, forward-thinking, a time of social mobility and technical innovation, and much of this is true. But then, as now, every alteration to the cultural or physical landscape challenged the values or lifestyle of someone. In the remote communities of the Lakes, however, opposition was a minority view and most realised that improved communication with the rest of a rapidly-changing England would bring rewards.

In the 1830s the Lancaster and Carlisle Railway Company was charged with finding the best route to the north, and the people of Kendal were determined that they would not be bypassed. A vociferous campaign for a branch line began, raising considerable funds through shares, in the knowledge that crowds of visitors could revitalise the region. The poet laureate, however, wasn't keen.

> *Is there no nook of English ground secure*
> *From rash assault? Schemes of retirement sown*
> *In youth and mid the busy world kept pure*
> *As when their earliest flowers of hope were blown*
> *Must perish; - how they this blight endure?*
> *And must he too the ruthless change bemoan*
> *Who scorns a false utilitarian lure*
> *'Mid his paternal fields at random thrown?*
> *Baffle the threat, bright Scene, from Orresthead*

Given to the pausing traveller's rapturous glance:
Plead for thy peace, thou beautiful romance
Of nature; and, if human hearts be dead,
Speak, passing winds; ye torrents, with your strong
And constant voice, protest against the wrong.

The poet feared the consequences of easy access for those he called 'cheap trippers', and wrote - in prose, we must assume - to every official and dignitary with an interest, from Gladstone downwards. It made little difference, and the Kendal to Windermere Railway Act received Royal assent in 1845. Two years later the cheap trippers arrived, rods and all.

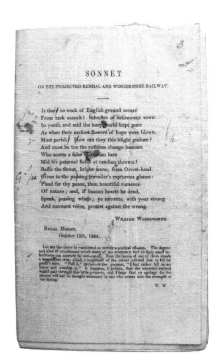

A proof copy of Wordsworth's sonnet about the projected Kendal and Windermere Railway, composed on 12th October 1844. Courtesy of the Wordsworth Trust.

Rumours were rife that a duplicitous Wordsworth had invested in the railway company and would make a tidy profit after all, but these were the whispers of local mischief-makers, and were never proven. The curmudgeonly poet may have had a partial victory, however. The line never did reach Troutbeck or Low Wood as intended, and visiting Victorian fishermen would have been obliged to travel the final miles by horse and carriage, or to have journeyed the length of the lake itself on one of the new steamers.

In 1893, Jenkinson's *Practical Guide to the Lakes* noted that 'omnibuses meet the trains at Bowness, and a conveyance from Low Wood also meets them. During the tourist season, coaches leave the station two or three times a day.' The cheap trippers had arrived, though Wordsworth's efforts had ensured that their final miles would be inconvenient ones forever more.

My own journey from Swindon, via Oxenholme and the Windermere branch line, entailed several long hours in a crowded Virgin Trains carriage. It was a Friday, and so I shared the airless and joyless metal box with commuters fleeing the capital for the weekend. I joined the

Trans Pennine Express train for the final miles, passing through Kendal and Burneside, and watched the landscape change in to the same vast and imposing skyline that would have intimidated the hardiest of Galloway Pony men. It was easy to understand Wordsworth's desire to keep such remote lands apart from the proletarian herds, and I might have stood shoulder-to-shoulder with him in defiance - had I not been one of those he wished to keep away.

When I arrived at the Sun Hotel at Troutbeck Bridge, late on that mid-June evening, the last thing on my mind was a long-dead poet with a fear of factory workers trampling down the daffodils. Like generations before me I was after the deepwater char. I was also chasing a forgotten tale about a giant pike and a young Joan Collins, but more of that later.

The bar at the Sun was full, and though it was too early in the year to be truly considered a summer evening, holidaymakers outnumbered the locals. The hotel was an impressive building, modestly-sized but in all other respects exhibiting the decorative grandeur that might have been expected by its Victorian patrons. Ornate slate and tapestry flooring led to a central staircase, and I wasn't surprised to learn from the barman that many believed the property was originally designed as a railway station. That may have been so, but of course the line had never reached it. He told me that an inn had been on the site since the 1700s, but that its fame had been secured locally only in the last decade of the following century when the landlord had been Thomas Longmire - a bobbin turner's son who befriended Charles Dickens and also became the undisputed Heavyweight Lakeland Wrestling Champion.

I was shown a photograph of the champ, and was genuinely impressed. Sepia images of long-gone pugilists almost always conform to a type - one photograph of a stocky moustached gentleman in vest and leggings looks much like another, after all. Longmire was unquestionably the genuine article, though, and reminded me that for all the grandeur of their architecture and fondness for social niceties, the Victorians still derived great pleasure from watching two grown men batter seven bells out of each other.

My presence in the bar attracted some attention, of a kind that was to become all too common during these journeys. A rucksack with fishing rods strapped to it has a magnetism of its own, and within minutes three of the locals had declared themselves as anglers. A round of drinks can be a smart investment at such times, and it was certainly so that evening in the Sun Hotel. I learnt of the recent recovery of the roach population, of the demise of the perch, and of the enormous pike that had been caught from the bank at Low Wood only weeks ago. I was told of the influx of chub and bream from one of the tarns in the hills, and the improved water quality since the banning of the speedboats. Suggested fly patterns for the brown trout were offered, and so too was use of a private lakeside launch ten minutes walk from where we stood. There was even some uncharacteristically frank discussion of the ferox trout population; it was only when I asked about the char fishing that I met with silence and shrugs.

This can happen when a visiting fisherman hits a raw nerve among the locals. I've come across the phenomenon before, in Ireland especially, and it always makes me think of the scene in *An American Werewolf in London* when one of the American backpackers asks about the satanic star scratched on the pub wall. There's a palpable change in the atmosphere, and the beer takes on a sudden chill.

When I mentioned char, the room didn't fall silent. The darts player didn't mutter 'you made me miss' and Brian Glover didn't materialise and show me the door. Nobody howled at the moon, but the recent expansiveness of my new fishing friends did evaporate, and the conversation turned to football. Char fishing, it seemed, was a local dark art, and I the overly curious outsider.

It didn't matter. I had a century-old char boat booked the following morning, and would learn whatever secrets needed to be learnt out on the water. I also had an old copy of *The English Lake District Fisheries* (1925 edition) by John Watson to rely upon, and this offered two entire chapters of char fishing lore. I finished my pint, and retired to bed with Watson's words for company - by breakfast, I would be an expert.

Watson's guide to the Lakes, typically for books of its age, focuses largely upon the game fishing in the region. Some coverage is given to the perch of the lakes, and of course to pike, but the author is ostensibly a fly fisherman, and the suggestion is implicit throughout that visiting anglers would have sought trout and salmon. That said, the char fishing - and the local industry linked to it - merit two chapters. According to the author, Windermere char had been netted for commercial purposes since the 1600s, and 'potted char' were much-prized in London. Decorated china pots of small fish, sealed in butter, were taken by the new rail system down to the capital overnight, as well as to hotels and inns in the north-west. At least one lakeside hostelry kept live char in metal containers so that customers could have fresh fish all year - at ten shillings a dozen, we are told. Watson suggests that by the mid-1800s, excessive netting had reduced the char stocks, and describes efforts at Wansfell to hatch char in boxes sunk in the lake's margins. Restrictions on netting were enforced in the 1870s, and so much of Watson's writing describes the local and highly-idiosyncratic method of catching char on rod and line - plumb-lining:

'*The weight, or plumb, is a cone with an elliptical base, weighing from 1½ to 2 lb, and having a feather of metal rudder to keep it from twisting. An average plumb-line consists of 26 yards of well-dressed stout line, to which are lashed six droppers or tail lines. The top dropper is five yards from the top of the line, the others following at intervals of four yards, while the bottom dropper is about a yards from the plumb. Each dropper terminates in a trace of medium lake gut, 3 yards in length. The baits are made of thin metal, so shaped that the wings or ears are on the principle of an Archimedean screw.*

Watson explains the need for long and powerful rods to carry the line and weight out from the boat, and the value of a bell on the end of each pole to identify a bite. He provides complex explanations of seven-part lines with tangle-defying swivels and rings, and the inclusion of pegs on the side of the boat on which to attach each section. Weighty paragraphs are devoted to the retrieval and storage of the plumb-line at the end of each troll.

In the early hours, and after a number of beers, it was

baffling stuff. By the time I put Watson's book down and turned off the light I had only four hours in which to dream fitfully of Archimedean screws before I was expected on the quay at Low Wood. There - just possibly - Watson's elaborate descriptions would begin to make a little sense.

The man charged with making sense of Watson's wordy proclamations was Tim Berry. Tim is one of the Directors of the Low Wood Hotel and its related businesses, and spends much of his life on or by Windermere. He is also one of a handful of men who keeps the tradition of plumb-lining alive on Windermere, and I had been told months before that a day on Tim's boat was something special. We met at dawn, in heavy rain. The wind was low and the lake calm, but the day promised to be a spectacularly wet one; this, it seemed, didn't matter - my host's enthusiasm was endless, and contagious, and within minutes his remarkable char boat was being lowered down the slipway on to Windermere.

Tim's boat - named Emily after one of his three daughters - dates back to 1910, and is an authentic char fishing design. Built entirely of wood in clinker fashion by apprentices at Borwicks Boat Yard, it is kitted out with pegs for securing the plumb-lines, and with two fifteen-foot poles with bells for taking out the lines. Tim told me that it was the apprentices who built the rowing boats on Windermere and only after years of doing so were they permitted to work on Windermere-class sailing vessels. The rowing boats were no mean achievement in themselves, though, and were designed with every angling comfort and necessity in mind.

Just before we left shore, Tim placed a square wooden

box in the boat. This, I would soon discover, held the lines and lures that are the props of the char-fisherman's dark magic. It was closed, and on its top was a plaque which read 'Please Knock'. This, Tim told me, was a reference to the bite - or knock - which would be signalled by a ringing bell.

"I purchased the boat around the time of my first daughter's birth," he remembered. "When I went to the Registrar's Office in Kendal Town Hall to register my daughter's birth, there was a gentleman unscrewing the 'Please Knock' sign from the door. My mind immediately turned to sitting in my boat on Windermere muttering 'please knock' to myself whilst waiting for the bells to ring. The sign was being replaced by a nasty plastic one, and I asked the man if I could have it - and he obliged. The Registrar was a bit miffed until I told him where it was going to end up."

Tim rowed first, taking us out in to a deep bay overlooked by the Langdale Pikes in the distance, and it became evident that this would be a day in which I would do little talking and a great deal of listening. Before we had reached the deep waters in which our lines would be dropped I had learned of Tim's family's long association with the hotel at Low Wood, of his love of the lake and all sports related to it, and of his desire to keep the char-fishing tradition alive. By lunchtime I would be equally familiar with his local youth and church work, his co-ownership of a salmon lodge in the Highlands and the fascinating life of his father.

My host's father, Michael Berry OBE, served in Singapore and Malaya in the 1950s, and after a decade in engineering took over the running of three hotels from his late uncle, Norman Buckley - a businessman and power-boat enthusiast who could number HRH King Hussein of Jordan, Donald Campbell and Richard Dimbleby among his closest friends . One of these hotels was Low Wood, the largest on Windermere, and Michael Berry set about making it bigger still. Conferencing facilities, new accommodation buildings and a fully-equipped marina were added during his Chairmanship, and Low Wood is now the most significant business in Windermere's tourist industry.

It wasn't always so; one hundred years ago, Low Wood was much smaller, but was internationally-renowned as a honeymoon destination, where the 'neogams' (newly-married couples, if your Greek is rusty) could enjoy famous views of the Pikes when they chose to emerge from the sumptuous rooms. Today's clientele, Tim told me, is more varied - watersports' enthusiasts mingle with royals and celebrities. The guest book at Low Wood reads like an alternative, and slightly bizarre, *Who's Who*: sundry British royals, speed-boat record-holders, the cream of Hollywood, poets, politicians, sports stars, Rolf Harris . . .

When the old man died in 2004, the running of the family business fell to Tim and his brother Simon, though it became clear during my morning's char fish-ing that such responsibilities did not prevent my host from living life to the full - I was, after all, afloat with a man whose business card describes him as 'Director of Fun'.

Two hundred yards out in to the lake, Tim announced that we were now over one hundred feet of water and could drop our rigs. The wooden box was finally opened to reveal the plumb-line itself - yards of thick braided cord, meticulously-coiled with nylon traces at regular intervals, attached by rings and swivels. At the end of each was a small polished metal spinner. These were broadly similar, with vanes and tails, though I couldn't vouch for their affinity to Archimedean screws. Tim attached a line to each pole, and dropped the entire ensemble in to Windermere's depths. A conventional spinning rod with a large Toby lure was cast behind the boat - 'in case there's a ferox or two hanging around' - and a slow morning of trolling began. When char fishing, this is apparently best undertaken by oars rather than outboard, and so Tim and I shared this duty as we covered the bay.

The char were elusive and the bells disinclined to ring, and our return for the morning would not have filled the smallest small char pot. That said, it was one of the more intriguing day's fishing I've experienced, and the company was excellent. As we returned to shore, Tim suggested that I try for pike and roach for the remainder of my stay. A thirty-pound pike had been caught in the margins behind Low Wood's marina only weeks before, and large shoals of roach could be found beneath the luxury cruisers at the hotel's private jetty. All I needed was the code for the security gate - and Tim was happy to provide this on the understanding that the code didn't make it in to this book.

It didn't.

The roach and pike would have to wait for a few hours, however. The rain had worsened, and the bar at the Sun beckoned. When I arrived, there were two men waiting to see me. Roger and his mate were char fishermen, and had been told about me by the landlord. Both, it seemed, were willing to talk. I was surprised at their candour after the reticence of other locals in the bar the previous evening, but these two had no such reservations and, helpfully, had sunk a couple of pints while waiting for my return.

Roger told of the prolific sport on Windermere in the early 1980s, of a recent dip in char numbers, and of the cyclical nature of such things. Both had lived on the water long enough to experience good years and bad, and to know the value of patience in lean times. Roger told me of his greatest day on Windermere - two four-hour trips in a day, catching sixty-two and sixty-three fish respectively. We spoke about the intricacies of lure shape, of the importance of polishing each spinner, and of local char fishing rivalries. Both men knew of local pubs and restaurants that would still buy a few char - invariably in cash, at the back door - if the captor was local and discreet, and both men were confident that the char fishing on Windermere would peak once again. While the locals waited for this, and it might take years, the pike and coarse fish kept the tourists happy.

We then left the pub to visit one of the men's houses, to look over his char fishing equipment. Once again there was a wooden box - this time, without a brass plaque - and inside it two plumb-lines carrying bull-nosed and bomb-shaped spinners cut from the lightest of metal. The rods themselves lay on top of the man's garage, the poles waterlogged and coated in moss, their bells rusted in to silence. He had not been afloat in a while, it seemed, but was waiting for the char to return in numbers.

I thanked both men for their generosity, wondering only briefly if their openness might lead to a late-night encounter with one of the local lycanthropes, and returned to the Sun to collect my pike and roach rods. I didn't have ten years to sit around waiting for char stocks to recover, and would be taking a train home the following day. I needed to catch a few fish.

It was June and I hadn't really come equipped to take on Windermere's famous monster pike, but Tim had given me a few spinners and jigs, and a rummage in the bottom of my rucksack had thrown up a rusting tangle of Mepps and Tobies. It was enough, and with a light spinning rod and chest waders I was able to explore the shallow margins close to Low Wood for three hours that evening. Little stirred at first but scattering fry soon gave away the presence of active predators as the light faded, and a rattling Big-S lure in silver conjured four takes. One came unstuck but the others came to hand - all pike, the largest perhaps ten pounds.

In the early morning, Tim's secret code gave me access to the hotel's private marina, and to shoals of roach. Thousands of redfins were gathered beneath luxury cruisers, and float-fished bread flake was seized on almost every cast. These were not big fish - from four ounces to almost a pound - but they were stunning, bright specimens. It was barely light, and their scales glowed. A woman on one of the larger cruisers soon appeared and queried my presence; I muttered Tim's name, which seemed to carry a certain potency, and continued fishing. Minutes later my interrogator, reassured that I was neither a poacher nor a well-disguised boat-thief, brought me a bacon sandwich and a mug of tea, and told me that there had been a pike skulking near her boat the day before. It was, she told me, over four feet long.

The roach drifted under the boats when the sun rose and bites slowed up, and so I walked back to the shore-front office at Low Wood to return Tim's pike lures. I had a bus to catch to Windermere, and then a long train journey south to Wiltshire, but before I left the jetty there was one last fish to see. It was a giant pike, badly-fashioned in fibre-glass, and was hanging like a highwayman from a gibbet at Low Wood's offices.

In the wake of the success of Peter Benchley's *Jaws* in the Seventies, Mancunian author Cliff Twemlow wrote a book about a giant pike in Lake Windermere, intend-ing it as a screenplay. I had read the book as a young boy. Brother Chris and I had the paperback, and were young enough not to recognise its derivative style - we loved it. (Twemlow always maintained that he started writing *The Pike* two years before *Jaws* was published in 1974, even though *The Pike* wasn't actually published until 1982.) In the same year, Twemlow and his backers arrived at Low Wood to begin filming their sure-fire hit, with co-stars Jack Hedley and Joan Collins in attendance. The open-ing scene was set up - a lone fisherman was to be pulled in to a bloody, boiling froth, leaving only his hat, floating on the lake's surface . . .

Sadly, the motorised pike refused to work, and the hapless author was forced to swim beneath it as camera-men struggled to control their mirth. The lone fisherman survived after all, and within weeks the proj-ect was abandoned. Joan returned to *Dynasty*, and would spend the next decade wearing excessive shoulder pads. The giant pike stayed behind, ignominiously strung up for the amusement of anglers and windsurfers, and there it remains. There is a photograph in the Douglas Dale Collection showing the pike being caressed by the divine Miss Collins, shortly before Hollywood thought better of it all - both wear fixed toothy grins, and neither looks overly impressed.

The pike has doubtless been photographed thousands of times since its brief film career, and on that summer morning I added to the number. As I did so, a small queue assembled behind me to do the same. This was no ordinary giant fibre-glass pike, after all. This one had been embraced by The Bitch, and belonged in its own obscure backwater of cinematic history - and fishermen and tourists love that sort of thing.

Perhaps Wordsworth had a point about his 'cheap trippers' after all.

The journey home was more leisurely, and I had a carriage to myself for much of it. Tim had presented me with a book on my departure, his father's history of the Low Wood Hotel, and I was able to put my feet up with an acceptable Virgin Trains latte and read. Joan and her pike were in there, and so too was a detailed account of Wordsworth's efforts to keep the masses away from the Lakes. The colourful history of Windermere was there too - the wartime requisitioning of its waters by the Sunderland Flying Boat Company, the controversial arrival of the charabancs, the era of speed-boat records and old rivalries between the steamers.

Little mention is made of the fishing, and this speaks volumes; Windermere is, and has been for two hundred years, all things to all visitors. Throughout its history, the fishing has remained a secondary attraction, and the potential untapped. On the previous morning Tim and I had watched large wild trout rising freely close to the boat. Later I had plundered shoals of roach that had, I suspect, never seen a baited hook before. Even among the kiss-me-quick ugliness of Bowness there is no tackle shop to exploit the unwary. Perhaps only in the glory days of commercial char fishing did Windermere give up its bounty to excess. I had read before about the perchine industry during war-time rationing, when the lake's perch had been canned like sardines to bolster nutrition on the Home Front, but even that had been somewhat of a damp squib - sales were poor, and no one I spoke to during my stay seemed to know much about it. If Wordworth's campaign amounted to anything in the long term, it kept the lake's treasures at a distance from the relentless march of angling progress. With the possible exception of the pike, which continue to attract trophy-hunters in numbers, the fish of Windermere have escaped the tourist anglers in this century and the last, and that may be regarded as good news - for them, for the locals in the bar at the Sun, and for dead poets too.

Chapter X

The Broads

If you mention Norfolk or Suffolk to anyone from elsewhere in England, there is a better than even chance that they will frown and say something like 'ooh, it's very flat you know'. Few will mention the stark beauty, the low population density, the windmills, the excellent fishing or the remarkable human endeavour that turned the land between the rivers Bure and Waveney into a maze of stillwaters. No, when it comes to East Anglia, we develop a sudden and overriding interest in regional topography. It's very odd.

The travelling anglers of the last hundred years knew better. They gathered at Liverpool Street station in their thousands through summer and winter, aware that they could leave the city and be among great shoals or roach and bream, or fishing for giant pike, within a few hours. Long before John Wilson and John Bailey wrote about Norfolk and made television programmes about its fishing, English anglers knew the names of its great waterways - the rivers Bure, Waveney, Wensum and Thurne, Hickling and Oulton Broads, Horsey Mere, the inter-connected expanses of Ormesby. Each had a reputation for a particular species, and the railways brought specimen hunters and pleasure anglers in great numbers to each of them.

Before the post-war boom in overseas travel, East Anglia was also one of England's favourite holiday destinations, and so the crowds on the platforms at Liverpool Street included wives and children too. Until the 1970s, no Norfolk or Suffolk tourist brochure was complete unless it featured a picture of a family aboard a small rented boat or cruiser, with at least one fishing rod in view. These garish adverts invariably depicted a cloudless summer idyll, but I was more interested in catching fish and so decided to go in October.

We chose to go to Oulton Broad, for no better reason than it is the closest genuine broad to Wiltshire and is still well served by the railway companies. Oulton is in Suffolk but has always been included in the generic term 'Norfolk Broads'. It is also just a mile away from the old fishing port and holiday town of Lowestoft, and would have been tremendously popular with visitors - many of whom would have booked their cruisers or chalets through W. B. Hoseasons, the holiday empire that was founded on its banks at the end of the Second World War.

I had two old guides for assistance - *Angling in Norfolk and Suffolk* by Bill Cooper (1956) and *Fishing the Norfolk Broads* by Peter Collins (1967). Both were aimed squarely at the holiday angler, and the older of the two even offered a glossary of local terms useful to visitors. And so, before we had even left the platform at Chippenham, Vic and I knew that *rokey* meant foggy, *slads* were pools of receding flood water and *Rodger's Blast* was nothing more sinister than a sudden gust of wind. We knew too that Oulton's fame was built on catches of gigantic perch. Bill Cooper had the following to say:

Oulton Broad, on the river Waveney, extends over approximately 132 acres. It is mostly from 4-5 ft deep, though deeper in parts, with a good bottom which is gravel in places. It provides excellent fishing and is noted for its big perch. One caught here weighed 4lb. 11 ½ oz. and many of 3 - 3 ½ lb have been taken. Pike up to 31 lb have been known, although not officially recorded, but one of 25 lb was taken in 1956 and there are also fine roach and bream.

Peter Collins' description was largely in agreement, but hinted that the broad was also capable of throwing up an occasional oddity:

As a perch fishery it stands supreme as the finest in the whole country. It is no flash-in-the-pan water; its reputation was won as a result of sustained catches of really big perch. The record for the 130-acre broad is the 4lb 12oz fish caught by Sid Baker of Norwich in 1962. It is a poor week that fails to provide anglers with at least one fish topping 3lb and a poor year when 4-pounders are not caught.

The broad is hard-bottomed and averages 6 ft in depth. It is not an ideal water for tench but in such a good mixed fishery anglers need never be surprised at what they will catch next. Before the last war one angler even caught a barbel here. How on earth such a fish, missing from the area as a whole, found its way on to Oulton is a matter for conjecture.

The relative shallowness of Oulton is typical. Few of the sixty-three broads are deeper than about twelve feet, and this is explained not only by the blandness of the landscape but also by the waterways' serendipitous formation. Early Roman settlers dug the eastern riverbanks for peat and by the Middle Ages a healthy local industry had emerged. Mediaeval monks, ever astute at fleecing the less worthy, ferried tonnes of the stuff to Norwich, Great Yarmouth and other districts. At some point unknown, the extensive excavations began to flood. Wind pumps and dykes were put to the task but were no match for rising sea levels and so, in the middle of the second millennium, the broads were formed. And yet, the crowds who came from Liverpool Street could not have known this; it was not until the 1960s that the true origins of the Norfolk Broads were established.

I called Lee Pullen, the owner of Oulton Broad Tackle, before we left Wiltshire and told him that we were coming to try for a big perch. He didn't fancy our chances. "In the old days, sure, but not now. They're not around in numbers any more and aren't as big as they used to be. You'd be better off trying for a pike, and they can be tricky too. Some days they feed, some days they don't."

It seemed that the perch disease of the 1970s hit Oulton as much as anywhere else, and its recovery has been partial at best. The summer visitors now fish for bream and silver fish, and in winter they fish for pike. I was secretly quite pleased about this; the Broads for me has always been synonymous with giant predators and I spent a disproportionate amount of my childhood staring at black-and-white photographs of record fish from places like Horsey Mere and Hickling. Lee told me that Oulton could be moody, but when the pike decided to feed there were 20-pounders to be had and he knew where they lived. Vic and I had a day in which to try and catch one.

We left Chippenham station - a Grade II listed building designed for GWR by J.H. Bertram in the 1850s - early on a Tuesday morning towards the end of October. The day was wet, squally and uninspiring, but I had been told that further east the forecast was better. The rest of the week promised high winds, perhaps even a few Rodger's Blasts, but little in the way of rain. I had left the perch rods at home and was equipped only for pike - this was a single-minded mission to land my own Broads monster and so the luggage rack above us creaked under the weight of heavy spinning rods, snap tackles and bungs, an overly-optimistic landing-net and a cooler bag stuffed with dead, frozen fish.

Remembering the disapproval engendered by my trout pellets during the Thames excursions, we left after the commuters had passed through and so the carriage that took us to London was quiet. It was only when we attempted to cross the capital, where every waking moment is part of someone's rush hour, that our unwieldy and slightly malodorous luggage became an inconvenience.

We reached Liverpool Street at midday, and I had been looking forward to seeing it. The station was built in 1874 on the site of the old Bedlam Hospital and was the first London building to be bombed by the Germans in the Great War. It was on the platforms of Liverpool Street that rioting crowds greeted the arrival of Joseph 'Elephant Man' Merrick in 1886, and where young

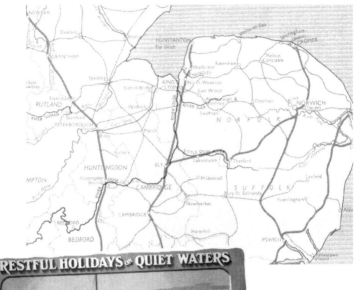

Top: Map of the LNER lines to Norfolk
and Suffolk in 1937. Before then, the
Great Eastern Railway and the Midland
& Great Northern Railways operated
services in the area.

Jewish evacuees from Europe arrived in the 1930s as part of the *Kindertransport* programme. The station had history, lots of it, but our stay was brief and the parts we saw seemed dank and unloved. Suddenly, the smell of the cooler bag didn't seem to matter.

The next part of the journey re-traced the route of the Victorian and Edwardian anglers, and as the train gathered speed I wondered what those old gents would have made of the 2012 Olympic stadiums being built alongside the tracks, or the post-industrial wasteland surrounding them. If they were relieved to have left the city behind, I knew how they felt. The landscape didn't appear to flatten unduly, but it did become greener.

We changed at Ipswich for the last leg, eventually joining a local rail network which has covered the Broads since the 1840s and is known as the Wherry Line. It took its name from the Norfolk Wherries, the boats which worked the waterways before the arrival of road and rail, but sadly, any sense of history has long disappeared.

Our carriage was a riot of blue plastic handrails, overflowing bins, grey tag-strewn walls and threadbare green seat covers, and the family sharing it with us took it in turns to disappear to the toilets and flout the smoking ban. Only once before had I been on a train as unremittingly grim. That had been many years before in Barcelona. My companions and I had been directed towards a carriage that included discarded needles and vomit, and so we had renamed it the 'Hepatitis Express'. The Ipswich to Lowestoft train was a distant second, but it was shameful all the same.

Our tickets were for Lowestoft, but we decided to escape at Oulton Broad South, a mile before the end of the line. The broad is served by two stations, North and South, on lines from Norwich and Ipswich respectively. Both were built in the middle of Victoria's century, and are found either side of Mutford Lock where the broad ends and the saline water of Lake Lothing begins. It was still raining when we arrived and Vic wanted coffee, so we shouldered our tackle and marched to the Wherry Hotel.

The *Where to Fish* guides of the 1930s often included advertisements for the Wherry Hotel, and when I had booked our room two weeks previously, I had asked the receptionist about its history. "Well, it is very old," she told me, "at least it looks very old . . . but the rooms are nice."

When Vic and I reached the bridge at Mutford, the hotel came in to view. Even in October drizzle, the Wherry was as impressive an example of Victorian opulence as I had seen on my travels. It sat on the northern shore of the broad, three storeys of red brick, white lead windows, slate roof and verandas, and from a distance it was beautiful. Only when we got inside did it become apparent that its grandeur had diminished over time. The décor harked back to the age of the Liverpool Street anglers, but little had been done to preserve it. In the Carvery, a solitary photograph from the 1880s hinted at a more illustrious past, but in all other respects this once-grand place was shabby. We finished our coffees, deposited the rods and dead fish in our small and curiously brown room, and walked in to town.

It may have been the miserable weather, or the aftershock of the final train journey, but we were not impressed by Lowestoft either. *Big Issue* sellers mingled with bored shoppers and the paved thoroughfare had been claimed by a listless gathering of 'goths' in eyeliner

Hoisting Sail, Oulton Broad.

and Marilyn Manson hoodies. A charity worker, one of the professional tabard-wearing variety that now seem to stalk every town centre, approached me as we entered one of the precincts. "Hey, dig the crazy beard, man. Can I talk to you about . . . ?"

We never did find out which organisation the tabard-wearer represented. My response to him was bluntly Anglo-Saxon, and Vic quickly ushered me towards a pub where beards were considered less remarkable.

We woke the following morning to warmer temperatures and a blue-grey sky. The broad was calm, untouched by rain. When Lee arrived to open his shop, a tongue-and-groove beach hut by the water's edge, we were there waiting for him. We chatted briefly, about how quiet trade had been and of recent rumours of a thirty-one-pound pike. The proprietor explained that the holiday fishers preferred the more northerly broads, and that other water sports prevailed on Oulton. For this reason, his boat-hiring colleague in the neighbouring hut would be charging us by the hour. "You'll not need long, though, if I show you where to catch them . . ."

He walked us down to the quay where our boat was waiting, pointing to the opposite shore of the North Bay and a rectangular cut next to the Wherry called the Dead End. "That's where they should be, if they're feeding," he said. "Good luck to you both."

Our vessel was a small, moulded fibreglass affair in red and white, but it came with a canopy and a small cabin, and that was enough to reassure Vic that we were not about to embark on yet another hellish journey. Ten minutes later, we moored up alongside a reed bed in the northern bay.

This was the first time I had been afloat on any of the broads. At first glance it differed little from the large waters I had fished in Cumbria, Ireland, Wales or the Scottish Highlands. Only the uniform shallow depth hinted that we were elsewhere - that, and the celebrated flatness of the landscape. Away from the Wherry and the bustle of Mutford Bridge, it was all quite wonderful.

Two baits, a herring and a smelt, were attached to the rods and fished close in. For an hour nothing stirred, and the wind began to get up. Vic hunkered down in the cabin to read *Broadcaster*, a free tourist paper, while I watched the floats and speculated on our chances of surviving one of Rodger's Blasts. Away from the quay and with a slight chop developing, our little boat now felt vulnerable, inadequate even.

By mid-morning, two gangs of pike fishers had chugged past on the way to the dyke, and I began to contemplate following them. Through my binoculars, they had looked knowledgeable, full of purpose. They hadn't stopped to even glance at the North Bay and they owned their own boats too. There was every chance that they knew where the pike *really* were. Just before despondency set in, one of my floats bobbed, slid sideways and promptly disappeared.

Our first Broads' pike weighed about ten pounds, but its size was immaterial. It was a deep, striking fish with a butter-coloured belly and pronounced green markings, and it fought tenaciously before coming to the net. The next came an hour later and was smaller but equally impressive. After returning it gently to the water I looked south-west towards the dyke, but the experts were nowhere to be seen.

Another hour passed without incident, and so we decided to return to the quay for a cup of tea. Lee met us as we pulled ashore and was delighted to hear that we had caught. "But before you go, you must try the Dead End," he insisted. "That's your best chance of a proper one." Fortified, we agreed that we would.

The Dead End was a rectangular bay, clearly man-made, a hundred yards long and perhaps fifty yards wide. On the western bank were moorings and industrial units, on the east the shore-front properties that are among the most-prized in Lowestoft. Each had a sign suggesting that anglers were not welcome, and so we tied the boat to mooring poles at the mouth of the bay, unclear whether we were entitled to be there. A cormorant skulked on one of them, and so we at least knew that there were fish around.

The afternoon wind turned and funnelled in to the Dead End, rocking our small craft. Rodger, it seemed, had finally arrived. The last of the clouds dissipated and as the light levels dropped we both began to shiver. At half-past three, Vic reminded me that the boat was due back very soon. I wound in one rod and tidied up, and as I did so the remaining float came alive. It bobbed three times, zipped to the right, bobbed again and then was still. I decided to wind down and see if one of Lee's monsters was sitting beneath it, munching on my herring. It was a lucky guess.

The last pike of the day was long and deep with wonderful olive markings and a head full of teeth, and weighed a little under twenty-one pounds. She had none of the bloatedness of a trout reservoir pike, none of the scratches or torn fins of an oft-caught warrior. Vic thought she was ugly but I knew she was remarkable. Above all, she was the kind of pike that would have attracted men from Liverpool Street in their thousands. She was a proper one.

That evening, we caught a train from Lowestoft and followed the Wherry Line to its source at Norwich Station. From there we took a direct train to Liverpool Street. Both were a considerable improvement on the one that had taken us to Oulton, and National Express East Anglia at last redeemed itself. From our clean and comfortable carriage, we were able to watch the Norfolk landscape disappear behind us as the sun finally set. It was all rather flat – and I decided that I liked it that way.

Chapter XI

Whitby

Until recently, I had only been to Yorkshire on two occasions. On the first, I sat in a corporate box at Elland Road, the guest of a Wiltshire-based Leeds United fan who had blown a lottery win on the men in white. We travelled up on a Saturday morning in his new MPV (registration plate L33DS), recalling the days of 'Sniffer' Clarke and Norman 'bites yer legs' Hunter, and lamenting the profligacy of the Ridsdale regime. As a Southampton fan I was there for the theatre and for the free lunch afforded to those who watched their football from the posh seats. My friend was there for the passion, the silky skills of young Alan Smith, the cut and thrust of the beautiful game - but the match was dour, especially so for the aristocrats who viewed it from behind glass. Nevertheless, the mighty Leeds were mighty enough, and did manage to beat Chelsea by two clear goals - which places that day in the very distant past.

On the second occasion, halfway through a circuitous drive to the Highlands, friends took me in to the Dales and to the Tan Hill Inn near Richmond, where we drank unholy quantities of Theakston's until it was time to leave. I supped my last, wobbled myself upright and battled with the arms of my coat.

"What in God's name are y'doing lad?" asked the barman.

I hadn't reckoned on the hardiness of northern drinkers or the lawlessness of their landlords. The curtains were pulled tightly shut, the door closed and bolted, and the Theakston's flowed on until morning. It was a memorable night - or so I am led to believe by those who can remember it.

But I had never fished in Yorkshire, or even thought about doing so, until the publisher suggested Whitby. I knew little of it, and imagined it to be a sub-arctic Southsea, all kiss-me-quick hats, bored donkeys, rolled up trousers and flat caps, but he told me I was wrong on all counts - not least because I would be going in February. It would be very different to the neon chaos of the Gaiety Bar but, if I was lucky, the cod just might be in. If they were not I would be doing something I hadn't done since my teens - flatty bashing.

Something else I had avoided since my youth was cheating at homework, but on the train to Leeds I did exactly that; lamentably, my hasty research on Whitby amounted to scanning a handful of old fishing guides and a bundle of printed pages from *Wikipedia*. The latter were surprisingly illuminating.

The first settlers were monks, who arrived in the seventh-century during the reign of Oswy, the Christian King of Northumbria. Abbess Hilda established a seat of learning on the high lands overlooking

Saltwick Bay, but two centuries of pious good were undone when Viking raiders arrived, destroying the abbey and changing the name of the place from Streonshal to Whitby. By the seventeenth century the town was a thriving centre for alum and shipbuilding, and in 1752 the first whaling ships left its docks. William Scoresby would become the town's most celebrated skipper and at the peak of its popularity twenty boats sailed out of Whitby, but the sinking of *The Phoenix* in 1836, in the shadow of the abbey, signalled the end of the industry locally. By then, the construction by George Hudson of railway lines from Pickering and York had brought tourists in great numbers. They have been there ever since.

The town sits in a deep valley at the mouth of the Esk, surrounded on all sides by cliffs and hills. Narrow lanes and fishermen's cottages recall its pre-Victorian heritage and the skeletal remains of the abbey overlook it all, but the coast hides a deeper, prehistoric past. Ammonites abound on the beaches and greater bounty survives in the hills, where fossilised pterodactyls have been found. The town has a literary reputation too, one which I doubted I would add to, and inspired the work of such luminaries as Bram Stoker, Lewis Carroll, Wilkie Collins and Elizabeth Gaskell.

The most celebrated Whitby artist of them all was not a writer but a photographer. Frank Meadow Sutcliffe was a Leeds man but settled in Whitby in 1875, setting up his own professional studio in a disused jet workshop in Waterloo Yard. Sutcliffe pioneered full plate wet collodion photography, using cumbersome equipment of mahogany and brass, complete with bellows. His work

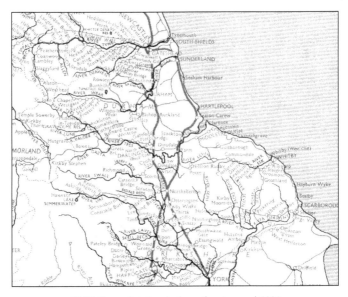

LNER lines and stations in the north-east, around 1937.

chronicled life at the port and among the jet workers, but it was his infamous 'The Water Rats' which outraged local clergy and saw him excommunicated from the church; the picture showed children in bathing suits messing with a dinghy, but these were chaste times and such wantonness - which today would be regarded as innocent and idyllic - was enough to darken his name among the godly.

By the time I arrived in Leeds, I considered myself a graduate of the *Wiki* school of hurried learning, an internet-taught expert - which of course is no kind of expert at all. No matter. I was there for the fishing, and on this subject my sources were beyond doubt.

Derek Fletcher's *Around the Coasts with Rod and Line* would have found its way in to many a tackle bag in the

days of the travelling angler. Fletcher, however, seemed
indifferent towards the sport at Whitby:

*At the mouth of the Esk, Whitby offers reasonable sea angling
from the harbour and piers. There is a lively club and an annual
festival usually in October with proceeds to the local branch of
the Missions to Seamen. Locals find best fishing from
September until late March when codling are feeding, but something is caught at most periods. In April and May one can hook
rock codling, billet, whiting and flounders. Bass too are sometimes taken by beach anglers, but for some time they were
thought to be shad. It caused great excitement in 1955 when
the club secretary properly identified one.*

Another source was a 1957 edition of *The Field*'s *Where
to Fish*. The Whitby entry was brief:

*Codling, sprag, coalfish, gurnard, whiting, cod and mackerel;
boat and quay fishing. The tunny fishing ground is off Whitby.
Further information from Clerk of the Council.*

I had no idea what a sprag might be, but I did know a
little of tunny. These giants arrived off the Scarborough
coast in the 1930s, and for two decades attracted the well-
heeled set - film stars, industrialists, society types and
high-ranking military heroes - to England's north-east
coast. The season peaked each year in August, when men
in dinghies followed the trawlers and, just occasionally,
hooked and landed fish in excess of five-hundred
pounds. It was a tremendously expensive business, not
least because the anglers had first to pay the trawlermen
to join in. Membership of the Tunny Club became as

desirable as a beat on the Test or a pavilion seat at Lords, and appealed to those who would otherwise have shown little interest in fishing or, indeed, a small town on the Yorkshire coast. Though Scarborough was unquestionably the centre of the tunny fishing universe, the deep water off Whitby was certainly part of the scene. But by the 1950s, its heyday was over and the mention in my *Where to Fish* was no more than a historic footnote. I knew that whatever I might catch on my north-east journey, it would not be a giant tuna.

The guides had more to say on the game fishing of the north-east. The salmon and trout of the Esk once offered prolific sport and a late-nineteenth century account in the *Yorkshire Weekly Post* had this to say:

The angling on the Esk is of the highest character. Salmon, sea trout and brown trout are sufficiently abundant in the river, and you can make good catches if only you can succeed in getting them out. This is not philosophy, it is simple statement of fact . . . if you stand in Whitby Station any night when the fresh-nets are on and see train after train disgorge its small contingent of anglers, each with a string of salmon thrown over his shoulder or a heavily-laden fishing bag, you will be satisfied that catches are made in actuality, and not in the corner of one's favourite smoke-room with an imaginative rod and line and a whisky-inspired cast of flies.

I changed at Leeds for the early train to Middlesbrough, relatively unimpressed with the view so far. The city appeared to have grown beyond all reason, and its grand and very large station was surrounded by high-rise offices, multiplexes, subways and a dual-carriageway bypass. Between it all were glimpses of a red-brick Victorian past, but its history appeared to have been swamped by relentless, marching progress. I had felt similarly on my day at Elland Road, and couldn't help but wonder what a doughty old curmudgeon like Billy Bremner would have made of it all.

I saw only platforms at Middlesbrough, but the final part of the journey was on the Esk Valley Line, and this improved my day immeasurably. We - and by 'we' I mean one fraught fisherman and countless half-term holiday-makers - passed through Marton, then Gypsy Lane and Nunthorpe and out in to the countryside. Urban sprawl gave way to ploughed fields full of opportunist pigeons, and the flat horizon began to undulate; by the time we had reached Great Ayton, it was all distinctly, beautifully Yorkshire.

The stations grew smaller and landscape wilder. My holidaying companions were a noisy and fractious collective, but a bright sky and the remarkable views gave our carriage the feel of a lively charabanc and, for once, I didn't mind the sticky-faced toddlers or their bickering parents. At Battersby we stopped, inexplicably, at an empty platform. No one got off or on. For a few minutes, nothing at all happened - and then we reversed back the way we came in to continue the route to the next station at Kildale. It was the kind of local, indulgent inefficiency that would have had Beeching muttering into his pink gin - and so I rather liked it.

Commondale and Castleton Moor stations came and went and then we stopped at quiet, timeless Danby, whose station was a traditional single-platform affair with an exquisite station-master's house - with the Esk at Duck Bridge only yards from its door. I had no way of knowing how many holiday trout fishers had disembarked there in the distant past for a week among the salmon and trout, purchasing their licenses at the Duke of Wellington and supping at its bar when sport ended each day, but I would bet that many hundreds did exactly that.

In the late-nineteenth century, holiday fishing on much of the Esk was difficult to obtain. Visitors could join the Esk Fishery Association and secure access to half of the river's twenty miles, but only if they could muster up £2 2s for an annual ticket. Danby, which offered good sport for a daily fee, would therefore have been a favoured spot for travelling fly fishermen. The remainder of the river belonged to men like Sir Charles Strickland and was, to use the quaint term of the day, 'preserved'.

Next was Lealholm, thought by many to be the prettiest village in Yorkshire, then Glaisdale, Egton and Grosmont. The line here links up with fabled North Yorkshire Moors Railway, with its steam trains running up to Pickering.

By the time we had reached Sleights and then Ruswarp, the Esk had captivated me. Its rapids and pools reminded me of the Averon, but the landscape around them was redolent of parts of the Upper Wye valley. I had never seen the river before, but I knew a little of it – not through *Wikipedia* this time, but through my old fishing guides and the archives of the *Whitby Gazette and Herald*. It was in the tidal reaches, in 1996, that England's last rod-caught burbot was rumoured to have been taken. The captor, a schoolboy, returned it without taking a photograph, but his description of a cod-like, eel-like fish has excited anglers and scientists ever since. This singular event, if it were to have happened at all, was good news for all who believed the burbot to have disappeared in the 1960s, and afforded Whitby a brief cache not seen since the days of the tunny.

If the river's notoriety comes from unconfirmed tales of *Lota lota*, its day-to-day reputation is only slightly less prosaic. The river has long been known for its fresh-water pearl mussels but a build-up of silt in the first decade of the new millennium has placed them in jeopardy. More recently, prodigious runs of sea-trout have hinted at a return to the days when, according to the *Yorkshire Weekly Post*, there were 'plenty of fish in the river and good panniers to be made'. But, whatever the fickle fortunes of its inhabitants might be, my first impressions of the Esk were only of its beauty.

My host was waiting for me when the train came to a final stop at Whitby. Phil Arnott was a friend of the publisher, but I knew his name from countless articles in the sea angling press. Among the weather-beaten, un-sentimental ranks of shore fishers, he has a reputation for knowing exactly what he is doing and doing it rather well; within moments of setting off in his 4x4, he was keen to establish my credentials.

"So," he asked. "Do you know what you're doing with a multiplier?"

I thought for a moment about childhood casting lessons and railway cuttings, about Mike and swearing and bloodied knuckles.

"Err, not so much," I said. "It's been a while."

Phil knew then that he would be doing the casting, and also that he was dealing with a feeble freshwater type

Whitby, looking towards the abbey, and below, the piers.

with precious little brine in his veins. We had yet to reach the water, but I had already been found out: just a fair-weather river man with a head full of *Wiki*.

We passed the ruins of the abbey and turned left towards the coast. Our first spot of the day was a rock mark, accessed by a cliff path whose descent amounted to one-hundred feet, but whose ascent would feel like a great deal more.

The Jurassic coast at Saltwick is remarkable. Heavy erosion has left blue-black jet strata exposed, sandwiched between thin limestone layers known locally as Top Jet Dogger. The shore is a tangle of boulders, but we trekked past these to exposed flats that looked to be slate, but probably were not. Our mark was at the promontory of this moonscape, close to a jutting needle of the same black rock which - if my O Level Geography serves me well - would be called a *stack*. Gulls hid in crevices and caves behind us, thousands of tiny sea creatures clung, like us, to the flats, and the relentless spray carried with it the cold winds of the North Sea. It was only by being there that the proper facts could be assimilated - the ones they don't write about on the websites. It was as dramatic a spot as I have ever fished.

Phil assembled two beachcasters, attached two tangle-some multipliers, and warned me that we were fishing over rough ground and would lose a few leads. "Wind in quickly and evenly and get the tackle off the bottom as fast as you can," he said. I grasped the unspoken subtext - *don't bugger about, you're not on the chuffin' Kennet now, lad*. It was quite a team talk - Cloughie and The Don would have been proud of him.

We fished with crab and mussel baits on simple pater-

nosters and, as Phil had anticipated, lost a few leads when
the tide swept our lines in to the rocks at our feet. Little
else happened, and the hoped-for lunge of a hungry cod
did not materialise. Three hours later, the incoming sea
had forced us back to the shore and we knew then that
the cod were not going to appear. Phil was not surprised,
given the colour of the water and mediocre height of the
tide that day, and so we rushed to the other end of
Whitby and to the more hospitable expanses of Sandsend.

"If you can't catch a flounder here, there's no hope for
you," Phil said.

I knew already that there was little hope for me as a
beach fisherman, but my host was optimistic and this was
contagious. The beach was busy; the last of the holidaymakers were packing up in the fading light and the night

Sandsend, in the days before its station was closed in 1958, even before Beeching.

shift of flatty bashers were assembling in the car park. Phil put two crab baits in to the third breaker and told me that the first nod-nod bites should be along shortly. He was right; our first enquiry came within minutes.

The flounder we caught that evening were not big. They were much the same as the ones I dragged unceremoniously from Fareham Creek in the 1980s (using, it must be said, a fixed-spool reel). Nonetheless, they were Yorkshire flatties and they saved a blank day.

As the natural light left us and was replaced by the neon of the hotels and arcades, we reeled in and handed our precious yards of sand over to the night shift. A small boy, perhaps ten years old, charged past me in to the surf and hurled his ragworm expertly in to the breakers. With a multiplier, of course.

The Middlesbrough train was running late and so I wandered down to Whitby harbour and its twin jetties. So much had changed since the days in which Sutcliffe had taken his evocative, sepia pictures. The sloops and schooners were gone and Belle Island, where Captain James Cook had loaded supplies on to *The Endeavour,* was now a car park. Nocturnal pier rats mingled with drinkers and tourists, but the Esk still flowed blackly and serenely in to the bay, as it always had. As the salty night air reached the back of my throat, I remembered the publisher's suggestion that I visit the best fish and chip shop in Yorkshire, and so I did. The queue outside the Magpie Café was testimony to its popularity but I was happy to wait, and my day ended triumphantly with a large Whitby cod after all.

Later, somewhere between Glaisdale and Lealholm, where the line followed the river and, just perhaps, uncaught burbot skulked in the silt, I decided that I liked Whitby very much indeed. By the time I reached Leeds, Yorkshire no longer meant just Theakstons and football to me. It meant flounder and limestone and the wonders of the Esk Valley too.

Chapter XII

Thank You, Doctor Beeching

Journeys have to end somewhere, and the last of mine took me to a quiet corner of Shropshire. It seemed appropriate; I could visit the publisher, celebrate the end of the project and remind him that our initial discussion - three years earlier - had alluded to 'expenses'. This did not require large bundles of used notes or extravagant cheques, and to be fair he had been more than generous with both in the past. No, I was more concerned with his seemingly endless supply of red wine and malt whisky. For the weary traveller, you understand.

The publisher knew just the place to cast my final line. Ellesmere was once famous among travelling anglers, and in the inter-war years the town's angling club even had a London agent who courted business among the capital's escapees. The region was known at the time as Shropshire's Lake District, in recognition of the nine glacial meres that have existed there since the last ice-age, and local angling clubs and railway companies were quick to capitalise on their long-held reputation for

CEREMONY OF

Cutting the First Sod

Of the OSWESTRY SECTION of the

OSWESTRY, ELLESMERE, & WHITCHURCH

RAILWAY,

On Thursday, the 4th September, 1862,

AT OSWESTRY.

COMMITTEE OF MANAGEMENT:

CHAIRMAN:—David Lloyd, Esq., Mayor of Oswestry.

Mr. Alderman Rogers	Mr. Councillor Dale	Mr. John Morris, builder
„ Alderman Morris	„ Councillor Saunders	„ David Ross, banker
„ Alderman Minshall	„ Councillor E. W. Thomas	Dr. Fuller
„ Councillor Phillips	„ Councillor John Thomas	Mr. I. F. Whitridge
„ Councillor Hilditch	„ Benjamin Roberts	„ Henry G. Weaver

TREASURER:—Mr. Henry Davies. | HON. SEC.:—Mr. Askew Roberts.

PROGRAMME:

THE DEMONSTRATION WILL BE COMMENCED AT 11 O'CLOCK IN THE MORNING, BY

A PROCESSION,

WHICH WILL

FORM ON THE BAILEY HEAD,

IN THE FOLLOWING ORDER:—

Brass Band.
King Oswald and Philanthropic Lodges of Odd-fellows.
Flags and Banners.
Band.
The Mayor and Corporation of Oswestry.
The Friends and Well-wishers.
The Railway Rifle Corps, headed by their Band.
The Directors, Officials, and Invited Guests.
Band.
The Court Duke of Cornwall Order of Foresters.
Flags and Banners.
The Ancient Briton Sun Friendly Society.
Drum and Fife Band.
The Juvenile Branch of Odd-fellows.
Flags and Banners.
The Children of the various Schools.
The Workmen.

The Friendly Societies will meet in the Horse Market, at Eleven o'clock, the Juvenile Lodge and the School Children on the Bailey Head, and the Friends and Well-wishers in the Powis Hall, so as to be marshalled in proper order to accompany the Mayor and Corporation from the Council Chamber, as the clock strikes Twelve.

The Procession will march down Bailey Street, through the Cross, up Church Street, down Lower Brook Street, where it will turn off opposite the Dispensary, along Salt Street to the New Church, and up Salop Road to the Cross Keys, and thence through the New Road to the SHELF BANK FIELD, where

THE FIRST SOD WILL BE CUT

By Miss KINCHANT, of Park Hall.

The Barrow and Spade will be presented by Mr. SAVIN, the Contractor, and after the ceremony, a few complimentary speeches will be delivered from the Platform erected for the occasion.

At the conclusion of the Ceremony, the Procession will again form, with the Foresters and Sun Friendly Societies in front, the Odd-fellows bringing up the rear. In returning, the Procession will march up Beatrice Street and Albion Hill, to the Bailey Head, where it will separate. The Children will then be supplied with buns, &c., in the Powis Hall. At THREE o'clock,

A COLD COLLATION

WILL TAKE PLACE ON THE

WYNNSTAY ARMS BOWLING GREEN, IN A SPLENDID MARQUEE,

Erected for the occasion, and to which the Ladies are specially invited to attend, as well as Gentlemen.

After the Luncheon a select number of toasts will be proposed and responded to, after which the Tent will be cleared for a

RURAL FETE,

To which the Luncheon Tickets will admit. The Admission to those who have not attended the Luncheon will be One Shilling, by tickets, which may be purchased at the Bar of the Hotel.

Tickets for the Collation, 5s. each, may be had from Mr. Baugh, Ellesmere; at the Bar of the Wynnstay Arms Hotel, or from the *Advertiser* Office, Bailey Head, Oswestry.

The Committee hope that the persons composing the Procession will assist in keeping to the order of the Programme, both in going to, and returning from, the field, so as to prevent confusion.

☞ It is particularly requested that Ladies and Gentlemen intending to purchase tickets for the Collation, will do so on or before Monday, the 1st of September, that the Committee may have some idea how many guests they will have to provide for.

SPECIAL NOTICE.—The poorer women of the town and neighbourhood will be provided with Tea in the Tent on the Bowling Green, on Friday, the 5th September. Tickets may be had from any member of the Committee.

ASKEW ROBERTS, PRINTER, BAILEY HEAD, OSWESTRY.

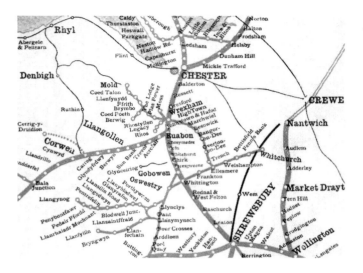

bream and other silver fish in the summer months and pike in the winter. But these were not what the publisher had in mind. "Get yourself to Trench Halt," he said. "You'll understand why when you get there."

This part of England was, until the 1960s, well-served by the emerging railway companies. Stations at Oswestry, Gobowen, Whitchurch and Ellesmere received brothers of the angle in considerable numbers, not only from the capital but from the large towns of the midlands and north. From each, branch lines took men in to the remoter parts of Flintshire and Denbighshire, weaving across the border into Wales and back again. The meres, rivers and streams were all within reach, and it was small wonder that anglers came from as far away as London to enjoy such tranquillity.

The nearest station to Ellesmere in the twenty-first century is Gobowen, and when I arrived there in the final week of the coarse fishing season, there were tangible reminders of its past. The Florentine stucco and turrets of 1846 have survived and, on the platform, posters announced a local campaign to afford it the protection of 'heritage railway' status. It was quite beautiful, in a Victorian, lost-England sort of way. It was busy too; Platform 1 bustled with passengers heading for Cardiff, Shrewsbury, Birmingham and London, while Platform 2 offered trains to Wrexham, Chester and Holyhead. It crossed my mind that if a new, coalition-era Beeching were to emerge from Whitehall with furrowed brow and calculator, Gobowen - if little else - ought to be safe.

Not all the Shropshire stations that served Victorian and Edwardian anglers have fared so well. Oswestry was the first of them to open, in 1848. Six years later, it was subsumed by the GWR monolith. The station building was chosen, in 1866, as the headquarters of the new Cambrian Railways, and its top floor given over to the company's board. Engines and rolling stock were repaired on site and the building itself was decorated in an extravagant Italianate style - for the people of Shropshire, it was their own Crewe or Swindon. But today, all this grandeur is gone. Oswestry station lasted a century but fell to Beeching's cuts in 1965. Now there is only a small museum, staffed by unpaid enthusiasts, to recall the glorious days of steam. The tracks have largely been lifted and the station building itself, though restored, is only partly used and partly boarded up. There was talk, among the men in the museum, of more restoration and regeneration, but as I walked along the remains of the platform that afternoon, I couldn't see it. The rusting rolling stock and empty shell of a building spoke of an age that was not forgotten, just relinquished.

It was pitiful, and so I decided to go fishing.

Ellesmere Station went the way of Oswestry in the same year, and so the final miles of my journey were, after much hanging around for buses that didn't arrive, completed in a taxi - whose driver was no more sympathetic towards my smelly rucksack than the commuters of the Thames Valley. It was then, in the final hours of all those railway journeys, that a kind of truth emerged. It is easier, in this new century, to travel to the international hotspots so beloved of 'destination anglers' - Tierra del Fuego, Cuba, the Kola Peninsula, the Fraser river and so on - than it is to catch a train through the English Midlands and go fishing. The mentality that provided the Victorians with their privilege tickets - early and late trains, vital but inefficient stations and third-class carriages - has morphed in to something else, something high-end and boutique. The honest majority, the soldiers of the taper lance who gathered at Euston and Liverpool Street to explore the waters of the provinces, have gone - and their place has been taken by big-earners in airport lounges with dorado and steelhead on their minds. By the time we arrived at Trench Halt, I didn't know whether to envy them or pity them.

So my curmudgeonly cabbie weaved through Ellesmere and took a northerly road out to where he thought Trench Halt should be. "There's a railway bridge and a cutting, and some lakes too I think," he said. "I'll drop you by the bridge."

Now I am very fond of railway cuttings. I grew up in Fareham in Hampshire and an abandoned cutting, all flint and high banks and buried sleepers, ran past the back of the woods behind our house. My brother and I knew it

A Wrexham to Ellesmere train at Bangor-on-Dee. © Ben Brooksbank. Licensed under the Creative Commons Licence. www.geograph.org.uk/photo/2614770

as a rich source of slow-worms which we trapped in jars and took home to an inevitable death, and also as the best place to practise beach-casting with our older neighbour, Mike. He was a teenager and owned an ABU Ambassador multiplier, and the cutting was where he took us for lessons in using it. Mike could hurl a torpedo-shaped lead over a hundred yards down its length, using what he called a pendulum cast. Brother Chris and I never perfected this, but we did become adept at silencing dog-walkers who encountered our casting lessons.

"You won't catch much 'ere, lads, ho ho ho. . ." they would say.

"*Faaaack* off, mate!" we would reply.

Unlike Mike's tanglesome multiplier, the dog-walkers of Fareham invariably did as they were told.

There was another benefit afforded to the wastrels of Fareham by the cutting - its steep slopes. This was before

BMX mania gripped the youth of England, but we had our own extreme sport and it was called 'bread-boarding'. Where the cutting met the main road at Gudgeheath Lane there was a Co-op, complete with bakery. The empty bread trays were piled up in the yard behind it and so we borrowed these and used them as sledges, sliding down the dry earth of the banks as quickly and dangerously as we could. With every run, slow-worms would dash for cover, the air would turn blue and, inevitably, the bakery staff would rush out and reclaim their trays.

And so I rather like railway cuttings, and can't pass them without thinking of beachcasters, 'slowies' and bad-tempered bakers. For that alone, Doctor Beeching, I am grateful.

The cabbie abandoned me on a bridge at Trench Halt and it soon became clear why the publisher had suggested it as a final, fitting location. To the south, a copse had reclaimed the land where tracks had once lain. Only the straightness of the tree-line hinted at the trains that had served the scattered communities between Ellesmere and Wrexham. But, to the north, the cutting was more easily-distinguished, and in the groove of earth dug out by navvies a hundred years earlier there was now a chain of lakes.

I already knew that the line had opened in 1895, and that it had been used for transporting munitions from the Royal Ordnance Factory at Marchwiel during the Second World War. I knew too that the service had operated passenger and freight trains until the 1960s when it had been judged inefficient and closed. But all the guide books and local historians had omitted one singular, crucial detail. In the hollows that Beeching left behind there were shoals of roach and bream and carp.

I bought my day ticket from the talkative farmer on whose land the lakes now sat. He told me that the fishery had been open for twenty-five years and was part of his family's expansion into the leisure industry - caravans, camping and a moto-cross track now surround the fishery. I learnt that in the three pools, each an acre or two and as straight as the tracks they had replaced, were carp to thirty pounds as well as all the delightful fishes now described dismissively as 'silvers'. I chose a swim at the bottom of the second pool and put up two rods - one for the carp, another for fish that I actually knew how to catch.

Now, I used to regard myself as a skilled, single-minded hunter of England's favourite fish. I owned a bivouac, knew the latest cunning rigs and could distinguish a Scopex boilie from a Tutti Frutti variant with my eyes shut. I talked in the language of the carp men - doubles, twenties, 'firties' - and sometimes I even caught them. But the lakes I fished became over-populated and some-how lost their sense of humour - if a lake can have such a thing - and I drifted away to the rivers and lochs. I followed the antics of the new breed of carp fanatics with fascination and admiration, but I didn't feel the urge to join them.

So it felt odd to be casting for carp once more and I knew, methodologically, that I was out of my depth. I also knew that corpulent mirrors did not belong in the era of the travelling angler whose steps I was trying to follow, but big carp are wonderful creatures and I had to have a go for them. The farmer suggested I try a 'zig rig' but I had no idea what he was talking about. I set up a link-ledger, with sweetcorn as bait, and it remained untouched all day.

My second rod was the one that caught all the fish. It was a simple float set-up, a waggler cocked using the only shotting pattern I know - an artless string of BBs bunched near the hook. The roach were ravenous and were happy to consume bread, corn and maggots in spite of the clumsy presentation. A shoal of small bream moved through the swim at one point in the afternoon, but at all other times it was roach after roach after roach. Most weighed a few ounces, some half-a-pound, and if I'd owned a keepnet it would have bulged by the end of the day. It was tremendous fun.

The carp and tench, whose existence I had come to doubt as the day wore on, finally appeared among bubbles and swirls in the centre of the pool as the light went, but I was just happy to have caught some modest fish. I was only a holiday angler, after all.

I left the publisher's house the following morning and took a last train home. We had drunk late in to the night, toasting the end of the journeys and flirting dangerously with wistfulness, nostalgia and the shameless wearing of rose-tinted spectacles. We agreed that Beeching had been a scoundrel with scant appreciation for the needs of the ordinary angler. We agreed too that 'destination fishing' had moved on rather too far since the days of the privilege tickets, both geographically and otherwise, and that the innocence of the days when men grabbed a Saturday morning train in search of smog-free sport in the provinces had a romance of its own. We knew, though, that this very era had been dominated by two world wars, by industrialisation and pollution, by the erosion of much that was dear, and that the charm of the riverside idyll was as much a construct of our imaginations as it was a reality of the time. The men who had lined the Thames on wicker baskets or cast their flies upon the Derbyshire Wye had lived in times as difficult as our own. They had been escaping too.

The journey from Gobowen to Chippenham was a slow one, all minor hold-ups and slight delays, but none of them really mattered. I had a hangover to lose and, as the coarse fishing season was coming to an end, several weeks to dry out before trout would begin supping at mayflies. I smiled at the memory of the small pools of the day before, at the quaint irony of an abandoned cutting that now provided such pleasant fishing, and remembered one of the discussions from the night before. The publisher had showed me a recent copy of the *Angling Times*; proposals for a high-speed rail link from London to Birmingham were threatening the landscape of Buckinghamshire, and more particularly the gravel pits at Denham - Savay, Harefield and others - that are the holy grail of modern carp fishers. It would be sad to see them disappear beneath iron and gravel, very sad indeed, but would echo events in the nineteenth-century when the construction of the railways doubtless displaced many fish and fishermen. The reasons were all too apparent from my carriage that day, and had been all along. From Lowestoft in the East to Vyrnwy in the West, the wilds of Cape Wrath in the North to the bustle of the southern beaches, the story is the same. We live on a small island covered in roads, railways and water. Britain's landscape depicts the ongoing conflict between our desire to get everywhere quickly and our fundamental need to be still - ideally, with rod in hand. Two hundred years after the revolution that created the dilemma, we are no closer to an answer.

The final miles of track that led to Wiltshire passed by great water - the Severn, the Warwickshire and Bristol Avons, countless pools and ponds. Each was a reminder of the days I'd enjoyed and of the wonderful fishing that exists still in every corner of Britain. Lily-fringed farm ponds, wind-swept gravel pits, rivers of every variety, beaches where the cod arrive as they should, piers where shoals of fish gather under neon and candy floss . . . we live in fortunate times.

The perennial complaint of every angler since Thomas Bastard, of declining fish and increasing fishermen, is as true and as meaningless as it ever was. Every generation opines for the apparently fish-rich days of its predecessors, but angling's golden age is then, now and tomorrow, if you know where to look. As I write, the first warmth of spring is in the air and the small stream near my door is beginning to sparkle with trout. Soon, I will be fishing for them. Perhaps in time I will venture further, and enjoy a day on the bigger river it feeds. And if I do, I may just take the train.